Published in 2023 by Hardie Grant Explore, an imprint of Hardie Grant Publishing, as a joint project with the Indigenous Literacy Foundation

Hardie Grant Explore (Melbourne)
Wurundjeri Country
Building 1, 658 Church Street
Richmond, Victoria 3121

Hardie Grant Explore (Sydney)
Gadigal Country
Level 7, 45 Jones Street
Ultimo, NSW 2007
www.hardiegrant.com/au/explore

Indigenous Literacy Foundation
Gadigal Country
Level 17, 207 Kent Street
Sydney, NSW 2000
www.ilf.org.au

The songs, stories and illustrations in this book contain traditional knowledge of the Tiwi people, and have been presented and published with the consent of the knowledge custodians. Dealing with any part of the knowledge for any purpose that has not been authorised may breach the customary laws of the Tiwi people and may also infringe copyright and moral rights under the Copyright Act 1968 (Australian Commonwealth).

The map in this publication incorporates data © Commonwealth of Australia (Geoscience Australia), 2006. Geoscience Australia has not evaluated the data as altered and incorporated within this publication, and therefore gives no warranty regarding accuracy, completeness, currency or suitability for any particular purpose.

Hardie Grant and the Indigenous Literacy Foundation (ILF) acknowledge First Nations People and recognise their continuing connection to Country, community and culture. In particular, we acknowledge the Traditional Owners of the Country on which we work, the Wurundjeri People of the Kulin Nation and the Gadigal People of the Eora Nation. We pay our respects to their Elders past and present, and honour the sharing of traditional stories passed down through generations.

A catalogue record for this book is available from the National Library of Australia

Murli Ia – Songs and stories of the Tiwi Islands
ISBN 9781741177992

10 9 8 7 6 5 4 3 2 1

Hardie Grant Explore

Publisher Melissa Kayser

Project editor Amanda Louey

Writer Dr Genevieve Campbell

Editor Bernadette Foley

Design and Typesetting Liz Seymour

Proofreader Gemma Taylor

Cartographer Emily Maffei

Production coordinator Jessica Harvie

Indigenous Literacy Foundation

Publishing Manager Kathy Mossop

Regional Coordinator, Tiwi Islands Tictac Moore

Colour reproduction by Splitting Image Colour Studio

Printed and bound in China by LEO Paper Products LTD.

CONTENTS

Canberra International Music Festival, 2021

YIPALA YINTANGA (FOREWORD)

Naki awarra ngirramini ngini ngarikuruwala kapi ngini-ngawula
   murrakupuni. Ngawa kukunari ngini awuta ngawa-ampi amintiya
ngawa-maninguwi kapi purumu api wuta warntirrarna mijiwaluwi
ngini putuwurimpura ngirramini ngini pitiripalamani kapi nginingawula pikaringini. Api ngawatuwu wiyi kapi ngawa pakajapuruwi
ngawurra-ngirimagi awarrra naki ngirramini ngini parlini. Ngawa-
jamuluwi amintiya ngawa ampi wuta waya ningani wurrani-ngurumagi
ngirramini ngini murruntawi pikaringini awanuwanga. Kapi
awurankuwi api pimataputurumi amintiya ngini wurra-ningirimagi
ngini-ngawula ngirramini kapi pikaringini ngini papaluwi
putuwurimpura. Awarra pupuni ngirramini. Awarra wurraningurimagi.
Ngawa ampi nginiwutawa putuwurrupurra awarra ngirraminni api
awarra ngawarra ningurimagi. Karri ngapaningimarri ngaruwanajirri
ngini ngarikirmi ngirraminni ngini ngawa ngarukuruwala.

*The songs in here come from all of our Traditional lands. This book is very
important for our community. You can say more in your own language. Our
children need to know English, of course, so they can move on into the world, but
they still need to know their own language so they will always feel strong and
proud about who they are, and so they can learn about where they come from. We
are determined to preserve our culture and our language before it is too late. We
want to get the young people interested in learning so they will keep the songs alive.
When they grow into young women and young men they will understand about
our culture. Wherever they go it will be with them. The knowledge our ancestors
left for us in the stories is something that we must hold on to. When we gather
around, we share together what is in the stories that we sing together.*

Ngarukuruwala Women's Group

Gemma, Regina, Nina and Marie-Carmel

Elizabeth, Ella, Anthea,
Ruth Helen, Katrina and
Frances Therese

MANY LIFETIMES OF SUNG KNOWLEDGE

Murli la is the culmination of many years, indeed many lifetimes, of sung knowledge. The songs presented in this book hold cultural, genealogical, geographical and spiritual knowledge that has been passed down through thousands of years of Tiwi storytelling, ceremony and in the songlines that circle the islands. The songs were composed over the past sixty years by a group of Tiwi women, who are known as the Strong Women in respect for their role as cultural and spiritual mentors, knowledge holders and Custodians of the old language and ceremonial poetry. The women have known each other since they were very young. Growing up in a small community, they went to school together, were mothers together and are now becoming Elders together. Through bloodlines and following kinship traditions, many of them also call themselves sisters.

The core group of women who sing today numbers around fifteen, and all have contributed to the songs in this collection in some way – whether as composers of new words, retellers of old stories though song or as the current holders of songs composed years ago by women who have since passed. As the generation of children that grew up in the crossover between traditional Tiwi ways and the era of colonialisation, the current senior Strong Women – now in their sixties, seventies and eighties – are unique in their understanding of past and present Tiwi identity. They know that, as it has always been, Tiwi identity is primarily held through the ceremonies that bring people together in the giving of thanks to the

ancestors, to Country and in respect and commemoration of passed knowledge holders.

As children, many of these women were separated from their families. They lived in the mission, removed from traditional instruction in language, ceremony and Tiwi culture. When they were little girls they sang as a group, first singing the hymns and nursery rhymes they learned from the nuns, then resetting some of those songs in their own language. As young women in the 1970s and '80s, they were active in the reclamation of self-determination and cultural sovereignty in their land. Having been empowered by English literacy and yet disconnected from their own language and culture, they became the first generation of Tiwi women to work in the school, the clinic, the shop and the art centres on the islands.

Feeling the responsibility and the pride of being the emerging holders of their deep-past cultural stories, songlines and dances, they reconnected with Elders and embraced the old ways, learning the stories and songs that underpin Tiwi culture. They actively created their own way of maintaining Tiwi knowledge and culture transmission, aware that they needed to sustain their community's connection to their Country and their ancestors.

The women are now the Elders and are called, with love and respect, the 'old ladies who know the songs'. They spend their days sitting together in the shade, weaving pandanus baskets, sometimes humming melodies so old no one knows who created them, or singing storytelling songs to teach their grandchildren about bush foods, the Palingarri (the deep-past times) or some wisdom of the ancestors. They are the Tiwi community's Custodians of the culture songs and mourning hymns needed for funerals. Often they will compose songwords and poetic phrases to mark a funeral, an anniversary of mourning or to help heal the next-of-kin. In the Tiwi way, each song is new for each occasion, and so the repertoire of lyrics and the body of oral record is vast.

Milika

The oldest senior songwomen in the group sing in ceremony alongside the senior songmen, taking central roles in leading the rituals required for the successful journey of the deceased to the next state of existence. They also enable mourners to fulfill their obligations of respect and to grieve and heal. In general, the songs are not written down. They are held by those individuals with authority, through lineages of kinship and Country. These people are the current Custodians of the songs that describe and name ancestors from the deep past, when the birds and animals were the tellers of stories and singers of knowledge. Those stories, words, places, names and actions are woven through fresh retellings of stories. The old words continue to be sung in new songs, carrying the teachings of the ancestors and drawing the generations together in an ongoing holding and passing on of cultural knowledge.

Maintaining the oral and interactive ways of passing on Tiwi culture is paramount for the Elders. They also recognise that sung knowledge should be preserved in written form, as the Tiwi language changes and as young people want to learn in new ways. The Strong Women started to compose the Tiwi words of their new songs in the 1990s. Incorporating poetic elements from the old language of their parents and grandparents, they composed new songs in simpler Tiwi language forms so they could tell the old stories to their children. The women's Modern Kuruwala songs ('kuruwala' means 'to sing') came to be synonymous with their generation.

Darwin Festival, 2017

The Tiwi Mothers' Club

From the 1970s to the late 1990s, women in a group called the Tiwi Mothers' Club organised an eisteddfod – a local festival of choirs. The singers were arranged in family, collegial or Country groups to compose and perform new songs each year in competitive concerts that the whole town would attend. Even now, particular performances and certain prize-winning songs from these eisteddfods are remembered with pride by those who sang them, or by their descendants who now sing them as part of their cultural heritage.

While the women composed, practised and performed the songs for pleasure and fun, they also had a goal to preserve the words, stories and knowledge that they, as the emerging adult generation, were responsible for passing on. While keeping the classical Tiwi musical forms, melodies and patterns, the women added the guitar and choral harmonies they had learned as children from the nuns and later from the radio. These songs were, and still are, as important to Tiwi culture as the classical song forms performed for ceremony. They are empowering for their creators and performers as well.

The women's creation of the Kuruwala songs placed them in a partnership role with their men, who were also embracing a reconnection with, and recognition of, Tiwi culture. Senior women and men were often the 'brains trust' for spiritually important language and matters of culture in the women's choral songs. In turn, the collection of songs enriched the linguistic toolkit for young women and men as they stepped up to sing at ceremony.

In 1970, an amendment to the Crown Lands Ordinance acknowledged the Tiwi people's ownership of their traditional lands, and the community reclaimed the right to openly hold the traditional Tiwi ceremonies during funerals. This meant the young people could participate in these ceremonies too.

The songwomen are part of a larger group – the Wangatunga Strong Women. Wanga means 'truly' or 'really' and tunga is the bark basket belonging to and signifying women. Wangatunga is also a baby girl. The Wangatunga Strong Women's Group are the senior culture women, turned to as role models and cultural advisors in support and wellbeing for the women and girls in their community. Among them are painters, screenprint artists, weavers, educators, storytellers and experts in traditional bush medicines and foods.

These women, especially the old ladies, hold the oral knowledge of Tiwi culture and a core group are now the keepers of song. They are not really a choir in the sense of having weekly rehearsals, with a conductor and scheduled programs, but more of an entity connected by a shared skill.

They have always sung for local events, special occasions, for church and for ceremonies, and they play an important role in the community as mentors, healers and cultural Custodians. The sung form of ngari kuruwala (we sing), Ngarukuruwala, has become a collective noun to describe the women and to include senior songmen who join them in a way that says who they are: a group bound together through the action of singing, through their identity as singers and composers and as Custodians of a continuum of oral and aural connection with the land they belong to. The Strong Women's Group at the heart of Ngarukuruwala are who they are. As Regina says, 'That's just who we are, what we do. We sing. We are Ngarukuruwala.'

MURRAKUPUNI, COUNTRY

The Tiwi Islands sit at the meeting of the Timor and Arafura seas, about thirty kilometres north of the Australian mainland. They are about eighty kilometres north of Darwin, the closest city. Traditionally known as Yirrara Ratuwati (the Two Islands), they are home to one of the oldest continuous cultures in the world, as people have been living in the area for around forty thousand years. Comprising two large islands and nine smaller uninhabited islands, they have been separated from the Australian mainland for about nine thousand years. Back in that time, the sea levels rose to cover a land bridge that connected the islands to the south and east of today's Melville Island. Local knowledge passed down through thousands of years points to freshwater springs and rock features there that are now under the seawater.

There are numerous distinct landscapes across the islands, with their characteristics and features forming the essence of each Country and the people who identify with it.

The coastline changes as the make-up of the underlying earth changes too. Following the shore you'll find broad estuarine inlets and creeks lined with mangroves, then wide, white sandy beaches. Dotted around are rocky outcrops, small reefs, sand bars, wide bays and expanses of tidal flats. Beyond the beaches are tall coastal ridges with long curving cliffs, where the orange and white ochres are gathered. Leaving the coast and following the mud banks lined with mangroves, the water becomes

brackish, then the mangroves give way to grasses, areas of mallee scrub and tall, dense eucalypt forest. Rainwater feeds reeds and waterlilies in billabongs, and pandanus and cycads around the waterholes, which are connected by creeks to springs further inland.

Understanding the land and the animals that live on it is essential for the Tiwi. Knowing where the crocodiles nest and how far along a creek each reptile will venture can save lives, and the community keeps up to date on the crocodiles' movements as the rains come and go and the creek levels rise and fall.

The various places on the islands are significant for the Custodians of the Country. The Tiwi have an unbroken connection passed down through countless generations of ancestors who have fished the waters, foraged for mussel, pipi, crab, turtle egg and mangrove worm, and stalked the wallaby, possum or magpie goose. Songlines lead people to good hunting and fishing grounds, and to reliable sources of fresh water. They continue to be sung as Elders pass on location-specific knowledge to their young people.

Many natural landmarks around the islands are significant meeting places, navigation points or feature in ancient stories, and have become embedded in the sung oral history. They have become anthropomorphised as family, the direct ancestors of those who call those places their own. One of these is Pajuwapura, a striking rock formation in the shallows just off what is now called Rocky Point, in Wurangku Country on the west coast of Bathurst Island. Pajuwapura is the Yimunga (the name for skingroup clans) maternal ancestor of the Pungaluwila People in the Oyster clan, a subgroup of the Marntimapila (Stone) Yimunga. She looks out across the water towards Country and represents the thousands of years of direct connection Tiwi have to that place. People refer to her by the appropriate kinship term because she is family. You would greet her as ningtinganinga (aunty) if she was part of your father's maternal clan and he would call her yimpunga (sister).

The area around Nyarringari (Goose Creek), in the north of Melville

Island, belongs to people who call the Magpie Geese their ancestors. The creek water is the nourishing lifeblood of family songlines and the swampy marshlands visited by the geese along the creek are part of the identity of the clans who share their heritage with the area and its nature, just as the fish that swim around murrupiyanga (the reefs) are part of the clans. When people recognise that features of the place are their family, and the core of their lineage and identity, their sense of duty to look after that place is very strong. Rather than 'owning' land, Tiwi people are its Custodians; its keepers and protectors. They interact with the plants and animals as their ancestors did before them and know that they will pass on that Custodianship to the next generation.

Taracumbi

TIMOR WINGA

Mirrimpi
(Pirripatiriyi)

Imalu

Pitiramirra   Punapuyama

Wuluwunga

Rangini   Mungarruwu

Purrapinarli

Piniyanapi   Tuwayanga

Kulimpini

Warriyuwu   Wulunjuwu   Pupmi

Marrawu   Nimangirrawu

Walamajarra   Tuwanyanga   MARRIKAWUYANGA   Kilumiyimpini   MILIKAPITI

PIRLINGIMPI○   Matalawu

Tawujapi   Punata   Timrambu

Mulaya   MUNUPI   Marrikawuyanga

Pajuwapura   MALAWU   Arrinkuwu

Wangarruwu   Atawini Putiwini   Puputuwu   WULURANGKU

Maluwu   Kuluwaga

Pukijiyamaluwu   Purrupajinga   Yapalika   Taracumbi

Yipinuwurra   WURANGKU   Jipipinga

Atayuni   ·Wurangkuwu

Kaninga   Jinkirrirawu

Murnunampi   Mintika   Pawularitarra

Tupwangampi   Tumarripi   Myily ·Paru

Pawunapi Pumpuru   WURRUMIYANGA (NGUIU)○

Ampwanikiyiti   JIKILARU   Lakatirnapi

Jikilaru   Ulatunga   Marralayangimpi

Tangiyawu   Mawuntuwu   Nangutu   Yirripurlingayi

Japarrinapi Yawarlinga Kilimaraka   Artawini   Mirntawu Mukunuwa Tantipi Pirrami

Yinanapi

On this map are place names that have been passed down through many generations of knowledge holders in the songlines. Most denote not a specific place, but encompass the coastline, beach and adjacent mangroves; the creek, the waterhole and the fresh water spring it is filled from; or the headland ridge and the bushland it overlooks. Some are a lookout point, a reef, a cove or a rock formation that are kinship totems, or the location of significant ancestral stories. As well as these are the eight traditional Countries, whose borders are organic, and so we don't confine them with fixed lines. Some places are now outstations and bush camping spots that families visit. These places have been lived in and walked on and sung for many generations before us.

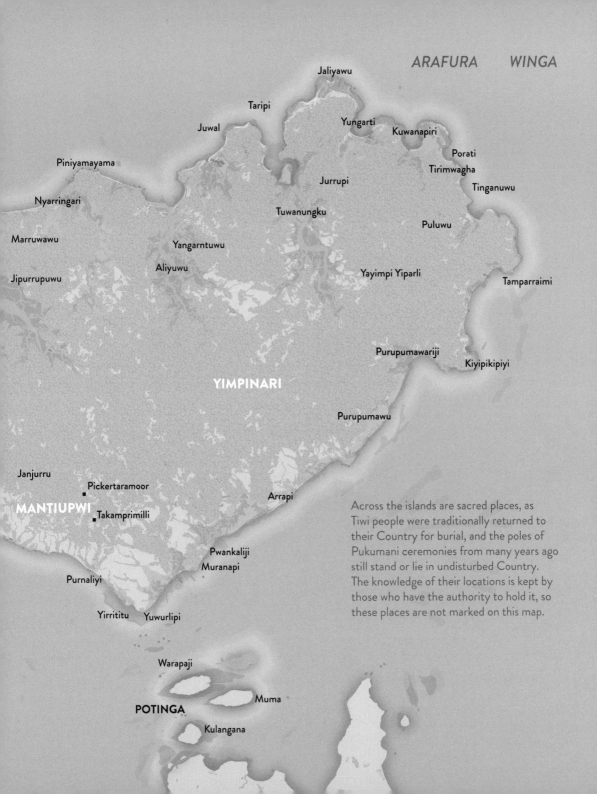

ARAFURA   WINGA

Jaliyawu

Taripi

Juwal   Yungarti
                              Kuwanapiri
Piniyamayama   Porati
                                 Tirimwagha
Nyarringari   Jurrupi   Tinganuwu

Marruwawu   Tuwanungku   Puluwu

Yangarntuwu
Aliyuwu   Yayimpi Yiparli
Jipurrupuwu   Tamparraimi

                            Purupumawariji
                                      Kiyipikipiyi
YIMPINARI

                    Purupumawu

Janjurru
    ▪ Pickertaramoor
                        Arrapi
MANTIUPWI
    ▪ Takamprimilli   Across the islands are sacred places, as
                            Tiwi people were traditionally returned to
                            their Country for burial, and the poles of
                            Pukumani ceremonies from many years ago
Purnaliyi   Pwankaliji   still stand or lie in undisturbed Country.
                    Muranapi   The knowledge of their locations is kept by
                                   those who have the authority to hold it, so
Yirrititu   Yuwurlipi   these places are not marked on this map.

            Warapaji

                    Muma
POTINGA

        Kulangana

Tiwi

'Tiwi' means 'people' and so 'Tiwi people' is really a tautology, but it has become standard when speaking in English. The term 'Tiwi' was how the people differentiated themselves from the animals and birds and the environment. The anthropologist Charles Hart coined the term 'the Tiwi' in the 1920s to refer to the inhabitants of the two islands. Before then, and indeed among the people today, Tiwi refer to themselves first by their Country and kinship identities. For example, Calista Kantilla, one of the Strong Women, calls herself a Wurangkuwila (a woman from Wurangku Country) and Lorringila because she belongs to the Lorrula (Stone) clan.

Calista

Until very recently in their millennia-long history, the people had no need for a national label because individuals only had contact with others who lived on the same island as they did. They were, to the best of their knowledge, alone in the world.

THE CREATION PERIOD

Passed down from the time back in the Palingarri, the deep past, the 'Dreaming' or 'Creation' stories tell how Murntankala created the islands and placed her children on them. Calista told us her story, and Concepta Milika Orsto translated it.

Parlingarri karri karrukuwapi purumuwu murrakupuni, api yartijanga yipingima nginingaji ngatawa murrualupuni apingimi. Karrikamini yirringarni, karlawu jupunyi, yirritji. Karlawu yanamurluwi, tokwampuwi, miputuwi, jarrakalani amintiya yirrikapayi.

Long ago there were no people on the earth and darkness covered the land. There were no hills or valleys or waterholes or creeks. No animals or birds, no fish or turtles or crocodiles.

Kuriyuwu kapi yuwunka purumuwu awuta yamparriparri. Yilaruwu murrakupuni jiyimuwu yinjula yintanga Murntankala, kapi nyirra mwaruwi Murupiyanga. Natinga wumunga niyrra papi jinirimi kapi awinyirra mupuka. Nyirra kularga jiyimi yinkiti amintiya kularlaga jiyama kapi yartipuranji ngini kapi pimantamajirripi nyirra mwaruwi. Karluwu wupunga, karluwu kukini.

*Above the sky were the Yamparriparri spirits and underneath the earth lived
an old woman called Murntankala and her three children. One day she dug
upwards through the earth and arrived on the land at that place Murupiyanga.
She looked around for food for her children and for soft ground where she could lay
them down, but there was no grass, no bushland, nothing.*

Murntankala jipamukurigi nyirra-mwaruwi yilaruwu kapi tunga kapi
jukwartanga kapi pirrartimarti ngini marruwapa awuta kakarijuwi.
Api nyirra jimarnuwa awungarruwu murrakupuni. Karri jimanuwa api
jiyikirimi yangamini kapi murruakupuni awinyirra mirripaka kalikali
yinipajimangimi kapani nyirra jukwartanga.
*Murntankala put her children in a basket and carried them on her back as
she was afraid of the Yamparriparri because they might want to eat her children.
Then she began to crawl around the earth and as she crawled along she made
tracks in the ground and the sea rushed in behind her.*

Waya piyaki kiyi awinyirra papi jiyimi kapi nyiraa pakinya
jipilikirimi, amintiya nyirra awungarra naki yirrara ratuwati.
*She crawled up and all around and back to where she started and she had
created these two islands.*

Palingarri was the time before the Tiwi people, when all the birds and
animals were the people, and when all the land was formed. The stories of
the Palingarri tell of how the ways to live, the laws, the beliefs and the lore
came to be. Many millenia later, the culture is one language and one
people. It is distinct from the mainland languages, music, art and beliefs.

Tokampinari was the time when life came onto the islands; it was the
time of the Tokampuwi (birds). The birds were the messengers, the
teachers and the dancers. For example, Purruti, the sea osprey, was a

fisherman; Mudati, the fork-tailed kite, helped discover fire. Jurukukuni, an owl, and his wife Pintoma performed the first Kulama ceremony; and the brahminy kite, Jankinaki, is the traditional caller and leader of Kulama. Men holding their own ceremony will paint up like Jankinaki, with white head and chest paint and brown ochre and ash on their arms. Kirilima, the jungle fowl, made the first milimika dance circle clearing and still builds his mound in that shape today.

Tokampinari is the dawn (literally 'the time of birds'), when the birds start to sing at first light. In the ancestral stories the birds and the animals taught the Tiwi, the people, the ways of ceremony, dancing and culture. The Dreaming stories (some of which are told in the songs in this book) tell of how their actions resulted in the ancestral people losing their human form and becoming the birds and animals we know today.

Birds continue to be messengers, as Japarrika, the Greater Frigate bird, congregates in large numbers onshore to warn of approaching storms.

The strait between the two islands

Tokwampini (Bird) was the father of Wayai, the wife of Purrukupali, the first man. He also was the teacher of all the laws and ways of living to be followed by the tribes across the islands. We will meet these birds in one of the songs.

Through their behaviours, tracks and calls, the birds continue to teach us about land care and nourishment, warn of weather events, and influence

Eugenie

the dance and rituals that they watch over as they have done for generations, since their own ancestors created these rituals.

Along with many stories in Australian Aboriginal lore, the Tiwi creation story of the old woman Murntankala recounts the creation of the Tiwi Islands. As the oceans increased and sea levels rose, the water came up in the channels gouged by Murntankala and the people became islanders.

At the time when Murntankala created the islands and left her children there to become the Tiwi, the Tokwampinari (the stories of Tiwi people) began. When the ancestors transformed themselves into the creatures, plants, stars and skies, they all became part of the skingroups, which continue to determine the Tiwi people's social and family systems. Today, the Tiwi embody the ancestors of their direct lineage, inherited through both their mothers and fathers, and manifested in the dances and songs of the Yoi (the totemic Dreamings) and the Yimunga.

VISITORS TO THE ISLANDS

Isolated and safe on their islands and with temperate climates, plentiful rainfall and abundant food resources, the Tiwi had little need to attempt crossing the open seas to their north, south or west, whose horizons showed no sign of another land. There are endemic timbers that would have been suitable to make lightweight canoes for fishing and hunting around the islands, but the open sea crossing was a larger undertaking and made only occasionally.

To the east and south-east are Potinga (the Vernon Islands) and the Coburg Peninsula, just visible in the distance. The local oral history tells of people sometimes making this crossing, and this is considered more likely once visitors began to arrive in canoes.

From at least the 17th century but probably earlier, Macassans and Malays made annual expeditions from the islands of the Indonesian Archipelago to the shallow waters of coastal Arnhem Land to collect trepang (the marine invertebrate *Holothuroidea*, also known as sea cucumber). Their route would have taken fishing boats close to the north-eastern coast of Melville Island. These trepang beds were not plentiful though, and Tiwi oral history and songs recount stories of strangers stopping for only short periods, mostly due to shipwreck, and of peaceful if sporadic contact.

The Tiwi were among the first Australians to have contact with visitors from Europe. Some old songs mention seeing sailing ships, called in Old Tiwi 'pirrawa' (most likely a borrowed word from Indonesian *perahu* and/ or Portuguese *prau*), in the distance. As well as these songs, there are written records of the presence of the Dutch and later British, French and Portuguese vessels in these waters, which are close to the sea trade and exploration routes of that era. From the late 16th century, the Dutch and the Portuguese would sail to Ambon and Banda, which they called the Spice Islands, in the Indonesian Archipelago, searching for trade and smooth sailing routes.

Dutch navigators mapped the continent's northern coastline, giving European names to the area we know as Arnhem Land and the far north of Western Australia. The Dutch merchant Pieterszoon, sailing close to the islands in 1635, sighted one island (much later called Melville) and noted seeing fires but no people. In 1644, on the return leg of his circumnavigation of the *Terra Australis Incognita*, Abel Tasman sailed along the northern coasts of the two islands, although he didn't realise

they were islands, presuming they were the top of the mainland. He reported seeing people on the beaches, so the Tiwi would certainly have seen the ship.

Dutch sailors wrote of their experiences during their explorations along the northern and eastern Tiwi coasts for about three months in 1705. They noted the sustained and mostly peaceful (though there was initial violence) contact with the people living around the Shark Bay area near Milikapiti, including Tiwi visits onboard the ship to exchange crabs and fish for knives and cloth. It was another century before Matthew Flinders chartered the two main islands in 1802. The navigator Phillip Parker King claimed them for Britian in 1819, and named them Bathurst (to the west) and Melville (the east).

Between 1824 and 1829, the British eked out an existence on the outpost of Fort Dundas, on the north-west coast of Melville Island. The fort was envisaged as a defence point and initially it was peopled with about a hundred and twenty convicts, soldiers and officers and their families. By all accounts, the relationship between the British and the

Marrikawuyanga

Tiwi was not successful, and there were attacks from both sides. Tiwi injuries, gunshot deaths and imprisonments have entered local oral history, and written history details the eventual abandonment of the settlement due to poor living conditions, the inability of the settlers to produce food, illness, disease and attacks from the islanders.

It was during this time that the British shipped buffalo across from Timor as beasts of burden and a source of food. When the British left, the buffalo quickly became feral and Robert (Joe) Copper was employed to go to Melville Island to shoot them for their hides. He brought with him a group of Iwaidja people from the Australian mainland. The following year, when shooting was paused to let the buffalo population renew, Cooper left for the Cobourg Peninsula on the mainland with eleven Tiwi adults and children. He returned in 1905 with another group of Iwaidja People and the Tiwi who had been taken ten years earlier. They set up a permanent base at Paru on Melville Island, where they remained until 1916.

Five of the Tiwi women married Iwaidja or Gagudju men, and so a number of Tiwi families today have close links with Iwaidja People and some Iwaidja loan-words have entered the language. The buffalo were left to run wild, becoming so characteristic of certain areas on Melville Island that Buffalo was incorporated into Tiwi culture as the totemic Yoi of tribes in those areas. Some of the Iwaidja dance Buffalo too, but the Tiwi are considered to be its Traditional Owners.

From the 1880s Japanese pearlers also started to visit the islands seasonally, and they set up a temporary base at the southern coast of Melville Island. The Tiwi had more regular contact with the Japanese pearlers during the 1920s and 1930s, until tensions leading to the outbreak of World War II saw the Australian Government intervene. The islands became the location of Allied posts, with a number of Tiwi men taking part in the war effort. As the 20th century brought more permanent contact with the outside world, Tiwi people have sought to balance new ways with respecting and maintaining the traditions of their ancestors.

CLAN AND COUNTRY

Maternal and Paternal Heritages

All Tiwi people pass through three states of existence – unborn, living, deceased – and these states exist concurrently. The Pitapitui (the not yet born) wait in Country until they are 'found' or 'sung' by their father, and then they are born. After living, a person becomes Mapurtiti and returns to their Country to join the world of the dead. The Tiwi living now, as the current Custodians, are responsible for looking after their Country so future generations of the unborn and the deceased are safe and happy in that Country. In various ways, the songs join these three states of existence together. When people call out to Country or when they sing at ceremony, they sing to and are heard by the unborn and the deceased. The songs join together the people who have lived, are living now and will one day live on Tiwi Murrakupuni, Country.

Every Tiwi person identifies with a Country, and with natural features, flora and fauna that hold significance to both their mother's and their father's kinship ancestors. Through their mother they inherit their skingroup totem and Yimunga, their clan. From their father they inherit their Yoi, their dance, their song and their Country.

Yoi

A Tiwi person's Yoi is their patrilineal identity and their connection to Country; the associated animal is the manifestation of the ancestral totem. The exact way that the unborn children (Pitapitui) are found so they can be born is impossible to explain, especially in English, but Elders say that a (future) father will sense his child by hearing them in the sounds of the Country, by dreaming of them or sensing their presence. The father might announce this by singing about them at ceremony or calling out to them – singing them into existence. This symbolic finding of the unborn child by the father is why people have their father's Yoi. Your Yoi is your inherent identity embodied in you as a direct continuation of the totemic ancestors from the Country in which you were dreamed.

If a child's father dances Crocodile, for example, then the child dances Crocodile, sings Crocodile, holds Custodial responsibility for the Country of their father's ancestors and for all the songlines and stories in that place.

Tiwi cultural practice has always embraced change, with the changing features of Country being incorporated into the culture and identity of its Custodians. This hereditary system of Country Custodianship and habitation assured sustainability of natural resources through generations of accumulated localised knowledge of the land. As extended family units evolved into tribes living in particular areas, an animal, flower or feature of the place became its totem. This system of Yoi, being intrinsically connected with Country, has seen the introduction of non-endemic totems in the past couple of centuries. Buffalo, Horse, Pig and Ship have become equally important patrilineal lineages, danced and sung at ceremony alongside those that symbolise Tiwi beings such as Shark, Crocodile, Rainbow or Jungle Fowl.

In English, Tiwi people refer to their Yoi also as their 'Dreaming', using the word that has come to describe generically the 'long ago' or the time of the ancestors in the creation stories of First Nations cultures. Tiwi texts in

Teresita dancing Tatuwali (Shark) with Jacinta and Regina at Tarntipi

English don't usually use the word 'Dreamtime'. While it's important to understand that for each First Nations culture there are different spiritualities, stories, explanations and understandings of this period, we use the term 'Dreaming' in this book knowing that it gives the reader a good idea of the essence of what it means.

The word 'Yoi' is used in many of the songs in this book. 'Yoi' means 'to dance', 'the dance' and 'the song that supports the dance'. It is also the gathering of people at a particular stage of ceremony, when they dance and sing their Yoi. This might seem confusing, but the best way to consider Yoi is as the embodiment of identity, through dance and song. When people dance at a funeral, a smoking, healing or Yiloti (Final ceremony), they are enacting their ancestral identity – Jungle Fowl, Crocodile, Dingo, Shark, Rainbow – with the song supporting them. In this way they pay their respects, connect to those around them and add themselves to the continuing line of those who dance and sing that Yoi.

Yimunga

'Yimunga' means the sun, the hour or time of day, one's spirit, life, breath and pulse.

Your Yimunga is your skingroup and clan, inherited from your mother. It is your essence; who you are deep inside.

There are four Tiwi maternal skingroups – Sun, Pandanus, Mullet and Stone. Each person belongs to one of these, and still today there are

important social protocols surrounding the relationship between them. The clans inside a skingroup determine who one can pair up with (sharing 'right skin') to start a family and create systems of reciprocal support obligations and allegiances. Within the four skingroups are smaller clan groups named for the flora and fauna associated with the Country their people identify with. Within Miyartiwi (Pandanus), for example, are the Tarnikuwi (Flying Fox), Mirripuwila (White Cockatoo) and Anjiluwi (Rain) People.

As they are matrilineal, these clans and subgroups align with various families through female ancestors, whom Tiwi people call grandmothers, mothers and sisters. The four skingroups and their sub-groups form a system of extended family, with the connections, responsibilities and support networks that go with it. When the old ladies sing, they speak of having yimingawama (good breath). From 'yiminga' and 'wama', meaning a lot or strong, this implies more than lung capacity or breath control in the singing sense. It means to be strong, to find one's voice, and be proud as a person when you sing.

'It also is to know who I am inside and where I belong and to sing that,' says senior songwoman, Jacinta Tipungwuti. This is at the heart of what song means to Tiwi people.

Through generations of family lineages and the movement of people across traditionally-owned Country, the Yoi associated with the families' senior men and the Yimunga clans from mothers create a rich and complex spiritual and physical connection with the land and the creatures in it. Songs often name Countries and clans. This is for acknowledgement and respect for passed family members and also to record the lineage of the performers, placing them and their songs into the songlines that trace around the islands.

THE CEREMONIES

There are, traditionally, two main ceremonial contexts for song in Tiwi culture: Pukumani and Kulama.

Pukumani

The word 'Pukumani' has a number of meanings, all related to the death of a person and the associated rituals. The deceased's name is Pukumani (not to be uttered), their image is Pukumani (not to be seen), the Country to which they belong is Pukumani (not to be visited), a song they composed is Pukumani (not to be sung) and the deceased's closest kin are said to be Pukumani (they are following the restrictions associated with mourning). It also refers to the overall state of a person affected by the death of a close relation.

What is generally known as the Pukumani ceremony is actually the culmination of a series of mortuary rituals. While Catholicism has elevated a person's funeral ceremony and/or Mass and burial to a more important position in Tiwi culture than it held previously, it remains just one of several rituals and ceremonies held for the deceased within the Pukumani process. After a person dies, their spirit remains in a state of waiting for about a year, or until all the seasons have gone around. Then they are released through their Yiloti (Final) Pukumani ceremony, and they join the realm of the deceased, the Mapurtiti, and become one of the

ancestors. The Yiloti ceremony of the Pukumani period allows Tiwi people to fully express and release their grief, to mark the close of the official mourning period. It is a public ceremony, bringing together extended kinship and clan groups. It also provides a forum for artistic expression through song, dance, sculpture and body painting.

The songs composed at Yiloti Pukumani, and at the funeral and associated sorrow and healing ceremonies, are as important as an acknowledgement of each person's relationship to the deceased, and through that to their ancestors, their Country, their Yoi and their Yimunga. The songs and dances of Pukumani all serve to aid the deceased's journey from their previous existence as a living Tiwi to their new one as a Mapurtiti. That new existence is not an end, but a continuation of one's presence. The Mapurtiti continue their daily activities and interactions with each other in the Country in which they have always belonged.

People worry that before their recently deceased loved one settles happily in their new existence with the Mapurtiti, they might not want to leave, or might want to take their living relatives with them into death. This is why, at mortuary ceremonies in particular, people disguise themselves with painted designs, ochred hair and beards, and make the air opaque with smoke in order to 'camouflage' themselves from the deceased. It is why the places the deceased had frequented, such as their home, the shop, their workplace or the social club are cleared of their presence and altered. The senior songmen and women do this by singing to the deceased about their changing status. People will also dance and 'mix up' the air with smouldering green-leaf white smoke, so that the deceased who hasn't yet been convinced to completely leave their mortal existence don't steal people away to be with them.

Once the smoking and healing rituals have been held and the songs and dances presented in the correct order, the deceased successfully makes their journey and are no longer tied to the mortal world. At the

end of the Yiloti Pukumani ceremony, the mourning period restrictions are lifted. Mourners can move on, knowing that their loved one has successfully moved on too.

Turtuni poles are the focal point of the Pukumani ceremony. They are made from the logs of the Kartukuni (*Erythrophleum chlorostachys*, ironwood), a tree that has great significance for Tiwi people because of its size, colour and the strength of its wood for carving.

These large carved and painted poles are created specifically for each ceremony and form the focal point of the ceremony, as mourners take it in turns to show their respect, acknowledge their kinship with the deceased and express their sorrow as they dance up towards the pole. Traditionally, the poles are placed in the deceased person's Country to represent the person and their return to Country, standing again as a new life in a different form. Since the introduction of Catholicism to the islands, Turtuni are often placed at the graveside in the town cemetery, and these days a photograph of the deceased might be the attached to the pole, signifying the lifting of restrictions.

Kulama

Kulama was important for spiritual, intellectual and personal growth into adulthood. The Kulama ceremony was an annual series of rituals primarily focused on initiation through the attainment of cultural and linguistic knowledge. Starting around their early teens, young Tiwi people were taught the skills for life – knowledge of Country, sky and sea; the seasons; hunting, fishing and fire management; medicine and safety; the customs, rules and responsibilities of gender, kinship and clan identity; art forms such as painting, weaving and sculpture; dance and spirituality. Kulama was not unlike school, with seven grades to progress through, year-round activities and rituals specific to each grade, and the annual Kulama ceremonies marking the students' attainment and

Dancing the Dreamings at the
National Gallery of Australia, 2021

'We learn our Dreaming dance straight away when we
can walk, you know? It is our identity from our fathers' side.
We teach our grandchildren now so they all dance too.'

Elizabeth Tipiloura

progression upwards. Much of this curriculum was taught through song, as the Kulama process also comprised schooling in language, poetry and music.

The ancient lore of the ancestors from the deep past and the symbolism of Tiwi spirituality were passed down from Elder to initiand, equipping them with the skills to embody the knowledge themselves as the next in the line of Custodianship and practice. Tiwi songs are not passed down word for word, and indeed singing someone else's song exactly is not appropriate. Each generation of singers learns from the previous one, and the knowledge, cultural information, ancestral names, places and stories are handed down. Through listening to Elders and learning the skills of melody and poetry, Tiwi singers aim to be able to compose their own songs to then pass on the stories and the knowledge in their own words. On learning the requisite grammatical, metrical, poetic and vocal skills, a person's status of 'full initiation' culminates in being confident, trusted and qualified to present their own song at Kulama as a participating adult member of their community.

Respect for Kulama remains central to Tiwi social and spiritual life. The surviving remnant of Kulama is the main ceremony, held annually over the course of three days and nights at the start of the dry season. It comprises numerous rituals: body painting, singing and dancing, as well as the cooking, washing and eating of otherwise poisonous native yams according to specified methods. Fully initiated men and women compose and perform songs and dances in order to ensure good health, community wellbeing and, most importantly, to ceremonially elevate young men and women through the series of initiation grades.

Kulama songs were a dynamic public record; they told of ancestral lineage, personal achievements and significant contemporary events. The Tiwi had no need for a printed register of births, deaths and marriages, honour roll, a newspaper, a bible or an almanac – all of this information was put into their songs. In an orderly process through ritual stages,

people commemorated recent deaths, named babies, negotiated inter-clan dealings, recorded storm damage or good fish catches, the sighting of a meteor or a ship on the horizon.

Everybody aspired to sing at Kulama as a matter of personal pride, and everyone was expected, when they were ready, to create their own song, satisfying various social, spiritual and socio-political needs. Within this framework, the songs of the Kulama ceremony were a vehicle for teaching, healing, reverence, social discourse, familial connection and artistic outlet, as well as an ongoing oral historical record. Some songs were composed to ensure spiritual equilibrium, while others were written for entertainment after the serious rituals were completed. In these songs, the singers' vocal or theatrical prowess, word play and humour were much admired and appreciated.

While much of the associated year-round ritual preparation for Kulama is no longer practised, a small group of Elders has kept the main annual Kulama ceremony alive. It is hoped that young people will start to learn this important ritual for the spiritual and social wellbeing of the community and themselves.

Some songs in this book are specific to an occasion or record a particular piece of social history. Creating a new form of songmaking that continues the ancestral traditions of knowledge transmission and record keeping, many of these songs function in much the same way as the traditional songs known as Ayipa. Sung on the third day of Kulama, Ayipa songs were an aural public noticeboard. Also called 'topical' or 'talk about' songs, their subject matter covered current events and items of novelty. These days, even as Kulama is less widely held, Ayipa are still sung at the end of Yiloti, the Final mortuary ceremonies, or at non-ceremonial occasions.

Among the Strong Women's Group's songs are many examples of the continuation of the Ayipa song function, and the women still compose them for any occasion they feel should be chronicled in the community's history. They composed, for example, a song for the arrival of the Olympic

Torch Relay in 2000, for a community Kidney Health Day, for the hundredth anniversary celebration of the mission, and a special song to open the Wellbeing Centre at Wurrumiyanga.

Many of these songs were by the nature of their function, one-offs – not recorded or written down. There's no reason to sing them again because they were for, and of, the moment at the time. In this book we have captured some of those songs that are useful for future reinvention (such as 'The Football Song', *see* p. 130), or have significant historical value (the 'Japanese Bombing of Darwin Song', *see* p. 146), but they are only a snapshot. The ladies continue to compose new songs for new stories all the time.

Nola

Tiwi Custodians say that as they sing the old words, they are learning from, adding to and passing on their accumulating cultural story and history. A recorded archive, such as this book, makes finite an artform that should ideally remain oral, changeable and intangible. In written form these words are set and tangible. However, they are also the starting point for new versions, as future song Custodians will add to them when they sing their own poetry, update information and include more ancestors' names. While we are recording and transcribing the old songs and creating an archive of audio and written knowledge, the current holders of that knowledge are all the while adding to it.

TIWI VISUAL ART

In their work, Tiwi artists continue the lineages of ancestral stories and kinship connections in the same way the songlines do. The connections between Tiwi songs, dances and visual art are strong, and the individual is central to all expressions of Tiwi culture and spirituality. Many of the songs in this book record the use of ceremonial artefacts – headdresses, armbands and spears – and many of the ancestral stories mentioned in them are also represented in the painted designs on ceremonial objects, carvings and other painted works from the past and in the contemporary art space.

Screenprinting

The hand-drawn and screenprinted fabrics used to make the Strong Women's dresses continue the cultural traditions, with designs representing Yoi, Yimunga, skingroups and ceremony. They also represent the sacred places; the birds, fish and animals; the skies and the flora of their traditional Country. When the ladies are preparing for a performance or a special occasion, they will have an outfit made in a design that is meaningful to them individually or as a group. Designs come in myriad colours, and the Strong Women's Group often looks like a rainbow as they enter a stage or a dance ground.

Painting up

Jilamara (painted) designs, have long been a symbol of Tiwi culture. The designs are associated with Yoi and Yiminga and are an important signifier of the kinship groups that bring people together. The clan and Country designs appear on ceremonial tunga and spears, and have been incorporated into contemporary art styles on canvas and bark.

In the days when initiation into adulthood comprised the years-long series of Kulama rituals, a great deal of time was spent painting intricate designs on an initiand's face and body. Depending on the Kulama stage the person was preparing for, these designs had to stay intact for weeks and so were repainted carefully during that time. Similarly, in periods of mourning and in the lead up to ceremonies, jilamara is applied by senior men and women appropriate to one's kinship relationship to the deceased.

Men and women will always paint up to perform at official community events. Children often wear their Yoi jilamara at special occasions, such as a school graduation.

The ochres in reds, yellows and oranges and the white clays used to paint the designs are sourced from select places around the islands. For body painting they are crushed and mixed with water, and for longer lasting artwork, the paste from the crushed stems of the Japartinga or Parlampalinga (*Cymbidium canaliculatum*, Tiger Orchid) are used to bind the ochres.

Tunga

The wangatunga or tunga is a broad, straight-sided vessel made from two solid panels of thick bark cut from the Jukwartirringa (*Eucalyptus tetrodonta*, Stringybark). During the wet season when the bark is flexible, the panels are stitched together using vine ropes and the joints are sealed with beeswax. Traditionally, women used tunga to carry bush foods they had collected and to carry items across a creek or waterhole.

To signify the end of a Final Pukumani ceremony, a painted tunga (when used in ceremony, it is called Imawalini) is placed upturned on the top of the largest standing Turtuni pole to symbolise the deceased's female ancestors and/or a deceased woman. The upended tungas also help to direct the spirits down into the ground of their Country, marked by the poles, rather than letting the spirits wander.

Pandanus

In every season the ladies carry out different tasks related to weaving – collecting Miyaringa (pandanus), splitting the long fronds into narrow strips, and dyeing, boiling and drying them. Then the fronds are ready to

Frances Therese collecting pandanus

weave into the circular stiches of the women's baskets. The women go to the pandanus groves that they have been visiting for years, allowing time between visits for new leaves to grow. These fresh fronds are the best for weaving. As the women walk through the dense eucalypt bush in search of the flash of bright green leaves among the greys, they call out to each other to stay in touch.

Once the fronds are split, small bundles of pandanus are coiled up and placed into tins of water to boil on a fire. Each of the women will dye her own fronds with various barks and roots, tending the boiling pots all day. Then the pandanus are spread out to dry in the sun, shrivelling into long, colourful threads ready to be woven. Although fine, pandanus is a strong material. Hard to break, easy to curl and with a sheen that gives the growing basket a

polished softness once the strands are tightly bound together, it is strong like culture.

'This one reminds me of Kulama [ceremony]. The outside part is the people all round, and the inside part is the Kulama–Milimika [ceremony circle]. We're all going to join in the Kulama ceremony – singing and dancing. The people all sitting around the Kulama, and this one is like different colours, people coming in, young and old, all celebrating the Kulama. They listen to the old people bringing their own song in,' says Frances Therese, while looking at a small woven pandanus circle.

There is a circularity in the weaving process that echoes the baskets themselves. Once the last strand is tied off and Frances sets a basket aside, she reaches again into her pile of pandanus and the circular pattern continues as the next basket begins to emerge. While the leaves are cut, dried and woven, the Miyaringa are regrowing, ready to be harvested again when more leaves for more threads are needed.

The women also weave the pandanus and feather pamajini armbands and japalingini headbands worn for ceremonies and special occasions.

Like those coiling strands of pandanus, songlines coil across the land, transporting ancestral stories along strands threading through generations, and weaving into new songs with new words, like new baskets with fresh dyes. The songs and the threads coil together.

Eunice

Marie Simplicia, Carol, Shirley and Lucinda
at Pirlingimpi front beach

SONG LANGUAGE

The language in which all ceremonial songs were, and still are, composed is based on the now obsolete language called 'Old Tiwi'. It was spoken across the islands before the arrival of non-Tiwi people in the 20th century. Old Tiwi is a rich and complex language, and different from any other Australian language. It is characterised as a poly-synthetic and agglutinative language, which means that it comprises very long words, made up of syllabic strings that denote tense, place, person, action, intent and even the time of the day, within complete words.

The art of Tiwi song composition further complicates the spoken language through the addition or deletion of syllables to fit words into regular metrical syllable groupings to suit specific melodies. Added to this is the individual singer's poetic creativity, using decoration, alliteration, metaphor and synonym. As well, singers will alter vowels to create aural colours, so that the vocal quality and shape of the words suit the intent and function of the song. As senior songwomen and men explain, sad songs sound like sorrow, songs for the morning sound like the morning and evening songs sound like that time near dusk. This feeling comes through in the words and also in the way the words are formed; the vowels and consonants are changed as they are sung, creating a level of language that is above normal everyday speech. It can be more poetic, more mannered and more florid.

As the old words are passed down and rephrased into new songs, the language has become, in a sense, archaic. As a comparison we might think about how English speakers approach the language of Shakespeare's plays. Using the old words in a song renders them special, clever and artistic. Tiwi song texts are highly poetic and involve multilayered allusions that build up as each song is passed on to the next generation of composers and listeners. The ability to compose songwords depends on fluency in the spoken form of the language as well as in the accumulated stories and cultural knowledge passed on through each generation of songwomen and men.

The ability to sing at ceremony was the domain of only the most senior men and women, and for Tiwi youth the mark of initiation into adulthood was the attainment of a certain level of song skills. When one was deemed

ready to compose one's own song for ceremony, one was ready to assume the responsibilities associated with being a full adult member of the community.

By the 1970s, a newer form of language, modified by contact with English and spoken by the Tiwi children, came into use. It was distinctly different from the old language spoken by the Elders. Through this contact with English and because non-Tiwi missionaries and school teachers used a vastly simplified grammar, Old Tiwi was replaced with 'Modern Tiwi'. It was picked up and spoken by all but the oldest speakers and those who lived beyond contact with the mission. Realising that the songs of ceremony and the stories of the Elders existed only in the old and fading language, the women found a way to bridge the divide by re-crafting songs in the Modern language forms. In this way, they continue to pass on the songs and the ancestral knowledge and stories in them.

Modern Tiwi has now largely been superseded by 'New Tiwi' or 'Apiniyapi' (half and half), spoken by young people and those under about fifty years of age. It includes numerous English loan words and syllabic, syntactic characteristics that make it almost impossible to utilise in the traditional Tiwi song forms.

Many of the phrases in the women's songs hold intact Old Tiwi songwords, poetic allusions and utterances of ancestral beings that were, and still are, sung in the classical ceremonial Tiwi song repertoire. Ceremony today also still requires the Old Tiwi words, which hold inherent cultural knowledge and acknowledgement of ancestral lineages, in order to properly mark the stages of the mourning rituals. The words in many of the songs in this book are no longer spoken and are therefore beyond the linguistic reach of most Tiwi people. Collecting them in written and audio form is one way the Strong Women hope to preserve both the poetry and the content held in their lyrics.

'I play and sing when we come together doing healing and singing.
That's how I do, every day under the shade. It makes me feel proud.
I do this every day of my life. When I hear my sisters' voices,
that's when I feel good.' **Augusta Punguatji**

Singing Culture

Almost every aspect of Tiwi culture – spiritual, historical, environmental and social – is referred to in song. Importantly, Tiwi songs are primarily new and contemporary. There are no 'fixed' or finite songs that can be learned by rote to be repeated exactly. Rather than having a body of songs passed down through the generations, it is the skill of creating one's own songs that is passed down. Due to this tradition of composition, retelling and invention, Tiwi songs form an oral, living public record.

Traditional Tiwi song practice is grounded on the notion of singing about what is happening at the time. The subject matter for the songs is either connected to kinship and Country, to ritual practice, or is topical, describing news or current events to the community and matters of interest to the audience. The fundamental notions of Tiwi identity, society and philosophy rely on the transmission of sung and embodied knowledge from each senior generation to the next.

Senior songwoman Jacinta Tipungwuti says, 'It was passing down from the old people. Passing down the knowledge they had. Passing down to us, and us, we are passing down our knowledge to next generation, ongoing.'

The songs in this book have been written down, but they are not rigid. Melodies, rhythms and words change a little as each new singer tells the story in their own way and for their own listeners. We hope these texts will be passed on to the next generations of Tiwi singers, who will in turn compose their own songs, telling the ongoing story of Tiwi people, culture and Country.

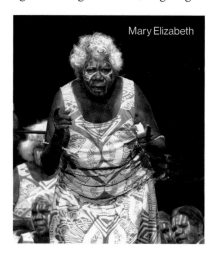

Mary Elizabeth

Kurukangawakawayi

Variations of kurukangawakawayi have been sung in almost all the women's performances and in ceremonial and secular Tiwi singing for as long as anyone can remember. It is the Tiwi equivalent of humming or '*la la la*', and added as a coda to extend the length of a song while people dance, or at the start of a song as an introduction to bring everyone together. It is also useful within a song if the following line is temporarily forgotten or the lead singer/composer is forming their words as they sing.

Kawakawani means 'sad singing' and kawakawayi means 'happy singing'. Kayai kayai, the 'crying words', are sung during the traditional widow songs at ceremony, and the old ladies will sometimes add those vocalisations to sorrow healing songs too.

The way these words are sung can change with each performance and each singer, and because there are no direct translations for them, we haven't included them in every song text, although you might hear them in the recording. Some of the songs do include kurukangawakawayi, or variations thereof, and we have noted them in those texts.

Ngirringani, father

Many Tiwi songs include references to ngirringani, which means 'father'. In the Tiwi kinship system, one's Yoi or totem – also known as one's 'Dreaming' – is inherited through one's father. Ngawa-ngirringani, 'our father', when sung by a kinship group, refers to the patrilineal ancestor.

Since the arrival of Catholicism, the words ngawa-ngirringani have also come to refer to 'our Father', God, especially in those songs that tell of the mission days or are sung in church. Other songs comprise much older stories and subjects and the words refer to family or to the ancestors of Country.

The words can mean either one's father or God, or both, to Tiwi singers; it depends on the time and place and occasion. We are happy for non-Tiwi listeners to hear in those words what they would like to hear.

The ancestors were the first Custodians of the Country and created all the lands people now call their homeland. The symbolism of the fathers creating the land, being around us and guiding us through Country can be heard with both Tiwi and Catholic cosmological allusions.

Spelling and translations

In this book we present each song slightly differently – some with direct translations and others with only a few English words that give the sense of the meaning. The Tiwi language was not written down until visitors made the first attempts to record it in the early 20th century. The various versions of orthography used since then mean there are different possible spellings, suggesting different pronunciations. The spelling in this book varies a little between the songs, and this indicates the age of those who collaborated to transcribe them and their opinions as to how words should be pronounced when sung.

Spellings vary. 'Turtle', for instance – jarrakalarni, tarrikalani; the word for 'peace' – ponki, pwanki; and the Country places – Tikelaru, Jikilaru, Tikelaruwu or Mantiyupi, Mandiupwi, Mantiupi. Older speakers still pronounce the word 'agha' (meaning 'oh dear') with the /gh/ sounding like the German /ch/ in *kuchen*, whereas younger speakers will pronounce it as 'aya', and so the spelling has changed too. Similarly, the 'The Football Song' (*see* p. 130) has as its title 'Yiloga' but within the text it is 'yilowa'. The g/w in this word is pronounced with a soft sound somewhere between the /gh/ sound and /w/. The spelling 'Yiloga' (really a misrepresentation of /gh/) has become the standard older way of spelling the word for 'bladder' or 'football'. Opinions differed too much to lock in either, so we used both.

Our first Ngarukuruwala performance. Darwin Festival, 2007

A Tiwi dictionary was compiled in the 1990s. However, as a fundamentally oral language whose derivations are in verbal transmission, and with living speakers and singers spanning eighty-five years of listening and utterance, it is best to see the spellings as guides and not absolute.

Some of these songs were composed by (now deceased) women in the group who were Elders fifty years ago, and so they include lyrics in the old song language that only the most senior singers still know and sing for ceremony. They hold the stories of ancestors, Country, kinship, seasons and social history from well before the arrival of non-Tiwi people on the islands. The complex procedures of alteration between the spoken and sung form to create a higher, poetic, artistic level of language was an intellectual skill that set song, ceremony and lore above the everyday. Fifty years ago, the women knew how special those words and stories were, and since then they have continued to incorporate 'hard words' into song language so that those phrases and words are not forgotten. To aid current and future Tiwi students of the song language, we decided that these long words remain, but with hyphenation to help distinguish each segment of the word. Other song texts group the words as they are sung, so the word breaks appear at different points from where they would be when spoken.

To give an idea of how these song texts are different from the spoken form, here is a breakdown of one line of the song 'Kupunyi, The Canoe Song' (*see* p.62). When we sing we change patterns of speech and shift emphasis from the way words would be spoken; in the 'traditional' or 'old way' of singing, the syllables are shifted, breaking the word groupings to create poetic, metrical groups of five, with one group of four syllables rounding off the line. To achieve this correct metrical pattern, syllables may be added, deleted or repeated depending on the length of each word and how they add up. Syllables are added (in parentheses) or deleted [in square brackets] from the spoken form, to fit the metre. The accents show the stressed syllables, another change from speech to singing.

SPOKEN

Pútupwarra áyikunji rrákiyángili wúmurupíyangírramíya
The tail of the dugong is flipping around on the water

TWO WAYS OF SINGING THIS LINE

Pútupwarrá(tu pwárra)[a]yikúnji [níkunjirráki] [yangilu] wúmurupíya
  ngírramiyá
Pútupwarrá(tu pwárra)[a]yikúnji [níkunji]rrákiyangilu wúmurupíya
  ngírramiyá

As the Strong Women brought the Old Tiwi language and their knowledge
of the old way of singing into their new song style, they continued to use
this poetic pattern and the melodic forms on which it is grounded. The
women do this, perhaps almost subconsciously, even when singing
non-Tiwi musical styles or melodies.

In the Canoe Song, within the Modern Tiwi lyrics is the Old Tiwi word
for dugong, 'rrakwiyangili'. Long fallen out of use in everyday speech,
rrakwiyangili now holds deeper Country and clan-associated meanings as
it signifies the places the dugong is found. The word only appears now in
songs, and its utterance draws together the people and the place in which
the story belongs. This song shows how much the words change when
spoken and sung, and the patterns of speech are radically altered. When
the women sing 'rrakwiyangili', the last vowel changes from /li/ to /lu/.
This is a feature of sung words, so they flow better. It is considered the
'proper' way of singing, and it relies on the old people's knowledge of the
origins of words from the very old songs that are
carried through into these new songs.

Not all Tiwi songwords and phrases can be directly translated, even
into Tiwi spoken or written form, and some concepts can't be expressed
satisfactorily in English. So in this book some lyrics are not translated. As
songwords, they are more than the story – they are part of the music and

Jacinta dancing
Yirrikipayi (crocodile),
and Francis

the time of the day and the place they describe. In the words are allusions to deep-past stories, people and places, with hidden meanings and symbolic references to skingroups, Country, clans and families, so the song texts transmit rich meaning beyond the face value of the words. Tiwi listeners will hear implied and associated meaning that is not wholly within the words themselves.

Some of the songs haven't been sung for many years, but we hope this book will help them come alive again and we will add to the recordings in the future.

Equality in Tiwi singing

The songs in this book were created by a group of women and so are now known as the women's songs. The book is a resource for everyone, though, and there are no restrictions on people of any gender or age in sharing in singing them. In ceremony, men and women dance in kinship groups in alternating turns – brothers, sisters, sons, daughters, fathers, mothers. There has always been a strong equality in Tiwi singing. In ceremonies held in mourning, for example, men and women dance and sing across genders and gender identities to ensure all the deceased's kinships are sung and danced. The acknowledgement of place and kinship and the responsibility of upholding songlines override any superficial distinctions between people. A senior man of a family might sing and dance the role of

'mother' if he is the closest relative on the deceased's mother's side of the family. A woman might sing in the voice of her male ancestor, depending on the patrilineal and matrilineal relationships to the deceased. As in many cultures, there are some song types that generally tend to be sung by men or by women.

The melodies

The songs in this book were composed by small groups of women, to be sung acapella or with guitar. Many have a sound that is perhaps not what we'd think of as 'traditional' or 'classical' Tiwi. Most of the songs are sung to very old melodies from specific Murrakupuni, Country groups. They were and, in some cases, still are performed in the traditional way: in unison, with a regular beat and with clapsticks. While the women have transposed them into the guitar and choral style as a way of making them 'modern', and perhaps more easily accessible for young people, the connections to Country through the old melodies remain as strong as ever. Women from the Country of each song are the Custodians, the leaders in performance, and the teachers of that song and its story. Some songs also exist in Kulama form, with the melody of its ritual context. Those songs are presented in text and in audio at the request of the senior women who still hold them.

Some songs use non-Tiwi melodies, borrowed from the radio or from songs the women learned in school. It is usually difficult to recognise those melodies because they have been changed by the different patterns of the Tiwi language. The chord progressions are more or less traceable to the non-Tiwi version but the changes, the symmetry, the phrasing and the tempo are so altered in their Tiwi versions that we certainly can't consider them 'covers'. 'Ngirramini ngini karri Piripini Murntawarrapijimi' (*see* p. 66) and 'Ten Guitars', for example, show that the source material of some of the borrowed melodies have no link to the Tiwi version. For others, the

subject matter of the original songs was the inspiration for the Tiwi version; 'Aya Ngirringani' (*see* p. 140) has a devotional intent, not so different from 'Ticket to Heaven', on which the melody is based. 'We Sing About Our Country' (*see* p. 184) borrows the melody from The Seekers' hit 'The Bush Girl'.

The Tiwi songs are not a translation of the original songs. Rather, the Tiwi lyrics are entirely new and tell Tiwi stories. It is simply a case of the women picking up inspiration from their aural environment. Just as the (pre-colonial) old melodies were heard in the bush, on the breeze or in the creeks, tunes on the radio seeped in to the women's aural consciousness, and they chose certain ones as the vehicle for their passing on of knowledge through song. In the same way as their ancestors picked up the sounds around them, the women created modern tunes from contemporary sounds to continue the tradition as Custodians of culture and storytelling.

As with all the songs, there is a feeling, a meaning that is in the melody. Whether a very old 'traditional' melody found in Country by the ancestors, or a relatively new one from fifty years ago, these songs are intrinsically connected to these women. The melodies are firmly connected to family, Country and to particular people.

Songlines and singers connect through time and in place, with all the songs telling of the ongoing interaction between the Elders and the young people to whom they are passing on their memories and knowledge, in an ever-accumulating body of cultural heritage and experience. Over the years and generations, some melodies have come to be associated with certain places and their Custodians. The 'Mantiyupi' tune, for example, is used by women who associate with Mantiyupi Country. This, and the melodies linked to other traditional countries, have become 'standards' upon which new lyrics are built. While some songs in this book are always performed to a particular tune, others have been performed over the years with different melodies, depending on the group of women singing them.

In the performance context the women maintain the traditional

practice of 'putting up' a song – a term used by senior songmen and women to refer to presenting a new song at a ceremony. This means that, even while following the structure and chord progressions of a well-known song, the lead singer will add her own words here and there, and the number of syllables and musical beats may change from line to line. This makes the performance a new retelling of the story, with the lead singer taking responsibility and cultural authority.

Rather than thinking in terms of 'bars' or 'measures', Tiwi singers count the number of syllables. This determines length of the phrase. Even when a song text is relatively fixed, the order of the lines will most likely change each time it is sung, as the lead singer (if there is one) or women in

Evening singalong, Wurrumiyanga

turn 'put up' a line that everyone knows and can join in with after the first word or so that acts as a cue. This creates an ensemble dynamic very similar to the traditional singing, where the leader singer/composer sings a line and repeats it until the group joins in.

Tiwi songs change each time they are sung, some a little and others entirely. This is because each singer is the current transmitter of the knowledge held in the song. The role of the Custodian of the inherent knowledge is to re-present to their audience (be they family at a funeral, students at Kulama or tourists at a concert) the elements of knowledge and story that are relevant and meaningful to the occasion. Words that can no longer be understood by anyone living are still sung, and carry on the associated sense of the person or place that they belong to. These very old words of ceremony now create the aural presence of ancestors, the calls of animals and the sounds of the land and the sea in ways that we can't really understand today.

As the Tiwi people traditionally hold their culture in non-written forms, the voice is a powerful vehicle for the transmission of knowledge through generations, and the sound of the Strong Women's voices is as important to the songs as are their lyrics. We hope that as you read the lyrics, you will listen to the songs via the QR code (*see* page 57), and enjoy the songwords for their poetry (whether you understand them all or not) and the knowledge of the Strong Women will be celebrated. Most of all, we hope this book will be *sung*. We encourage you to hum along when you can, and that those who do know the Tiwi language will use this book as a resource for learning the old words and to pick up the old ladies' songs so you can keep singing them yourself.

'It is important that we keep singing as a group of Strong Women.
We are getting older now but we always have good times together
when we perform and young people might join us and take over
one day and the stories will keep on going.' **Molly Munkara**

THE SONGS

Darwin Festival, 2014

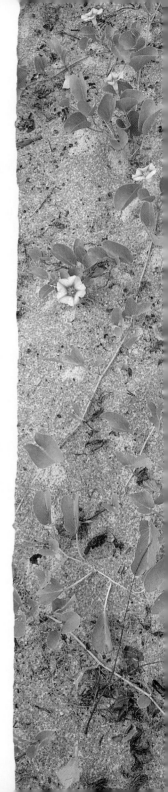

 You can
listen to the
songs here.

**All of the images accompanying the songs are
of the place, the design and the art of that song's
story and of the people who sing it.**

Old Murli la

A love song

When the oldest women were young, they heard the old ladies at Paru
sing the traditional love songs. Those songs were just for women, a bit like
gossip – about lovers or men they fancied. The old songs never explained
very much about what they got up to but hinted at their secret meetings or
desires. We composed a new version to sing as a group at our community
get togethers just for fun. Although we sometimes change the story a little
depending how we feel at the time, 'Murli la' is about a girl and a boy who
are in love but for some reason they can't be together. Maybe he lives on
the wrong side of the Strait, maybe he has the wrong skingroup, or maybe

Marcella

he has a girlfriend already. Even
though the words are simple, you
can imagine whatever love story
you want to and add your own
meaning, just like the old love
songs that have meaning
'between the lines'.

The words 'Murli la', which
are repeated throughout,
translate roughly as 'Let's (you
and me) go away together'. These
words can also express a longing
for someone in a friendship way. 'Murli la' has become a favourite of the
Strong Women's Group. We have performed it at music and language
conferences, public performances on the mainland and at local Tiwi
community events, as well as at Tiwi weddings.

Old Murli la

Ngiya nuka marringarru kangatawa turratuwula
I'm not going to the other side [of the Strait] because
*   I might get into trouble*

Piliwiya ngirramini ngikuntirrarri ngiya aghayi!
I might get in to trouble, people might talk!

Milalaya wantirraya ngimanikinawurrumi
I'm crying for you and I miss you

Kapi ngimparrimi muwiyati awarruwu
Wherever you go that's where I will go too

Ngimpata murrika ngimpata murrika
Don't leave me, don't run away

Murli murli la murli murli la
Let's go, come with me, let's keep on going together

1954 Love Song

Ngintangurriyu ngajimpatuwitawu
I'm sad that you are leaving this morning

Ngangilampuktangintu timinjimpaju
I send all my thoughts to you

Yitangi layitiwati minijirraki ningila
He gave me a torch to light my way

—Unidentified woman, recorded in 1954

Angawula Yiminga amintiya Yoi

Our Skingroups and Dreamings

Our Yiminga (skingroup) comes from our mother's side. It is who we are inside. Our heart and soul, our Country and our ancestors.

They represent the four essential elements of the world: the Sun (sky), Mullet (sea), Stone (earth) and Pandanus (plants).

The tunga (bark basket, pictured below) is the symbol for all women.

Ngirramini Ngini Tiwi Angawula Yiminga

Yirrara ratuwati ngawa Tiwi
The two islands of our people
Ngajingawula ngawa-rringani pirrimunjirroti
We come from our ancestors, our fathers in this homeland
Ngawatuwu awinyirra Yiminga
We all belong to our skingroup
Murtangimpila, Warntarringuwi, Marntimampila, Yirrikuwi
[The skingroups] Mullet, Sun, Stone, Pandanus

Ngawa-ampi, ngawa-rringanuwi
Ngawa-maninguwi, ngawa-naruwi
Ngawa-mwaruwi, ngawa-jamuluwi
Ngawa-mampi, ngawa-mamirampi
Our great, great ancestors, our fathers
our grandmothers, our mothers
our grandchildren, our daughters

Our Yoi, (Dreaming) comes from our father's side. It is our dance and our identity from our father's Country. Each Country has an animal or spirit totem ancestor and we dance that.

The walanka (spear, pictured below) is for all men.

Ngirramini ngini Tiwi angawula Yoi

Ngawatuwu awinyirra Yoi
We all belong to our Dreaming dance
Kitirika, Tatuwali, Pika, Kapala, Kirilima, Jarrangini,
    Yirrikapayi, Tuwiyika,
Turtle, Shark, Horse, Ship, Jungle Fowl, Buffalo, Crocodile, Whirlwind,
Nyarringari, Ampiji, Pikipiki, Taringa, Tayamini, Yingwati,
Goose, Rainbow, Pig, Snake, Dingo, Sugarbag,
Wunijaka, Nyingawi, Pakatiringa
Wind, Nyingawi people, Rain

Ngawatuwu awarra nginingawula yoyi
Each family sings their own song
Ngarra ngawa-rringani awarra ngawa yimintakirayi
Our ancestors gave us all of our culture and stories

Wurrikurrunyuwi, arlalinguwi wuta wiyi jilikari wujikurumayi
Young boys and young girls are keeping our culture strong through them

Yirrara ratuwati ngawa tiwi, ngari kuruwala kapi yoi
Our two islands of our people, we sing and we dance

Kupunyi

The Canoe Song

Men used to go out in their canoes hunting for turtle and dugong. First the canoes were made from stringybark, though later the men started to make dugout canoes after seeing the Macassans from the Indonesian Archipelago using them when they came looking for trepang. The Iwaidja people of Croker Island and the Cobourg Peninsula used them too. The word Kupunyi (canoe) is used by speakers of both Tiwi and the language of the Iwaidja people. Today, we still go out hunting to catch turtle and sometimes a dugong, but not in canoes anymore. These days we have motorboats.

Mirntati is a rock off the coast of Melville Island. It is associated with dugong and with the ancestors of those of us who sing about him. Another meaning for this line, 'Nginingaji-Mirntati-warangampiniwingirra-kiyangiluwu-miringarra' is 'He looks like a big stone – his back is smooth'. The rock is the ancestor, and the dugong is sometimes that rock too.

This song is from much older songs about dugong. We caught the old words from our grandparents to save in our song, so future generations will remember the proper way of singing the songs about our culture. Our new version uses an old melody that we also use for 'The Crocodile Man' (*see* p. 101). For 'Kupunyi' we make it a bit slower, swinging the words to go with our dance actions like the water lapping. The old words here have come from the traditional Kulama song about dugong, and so when we sing those old words we must treat them properly.

Kupunyi

Kupunyi-tarti wumpuningapi mikuji-rrakiyangiluwu-kuwularringi
Three men were paddling in a long canoe looking around

Pilamingarra purukunji-rrakiyangiluwu-munukumuni
The tail of the dugong is very big

Putupwarra-tupwarra-yikunji-rrakiyangilu wumurupiyangirramiya
The tail of the dugong is flipping around on the water

Nginingaji-Mirntati-warangampiniwingirra-kiyangiluwu-miringarra
The dugong is swimming around the stone in the sea

Piripati rrakiyangilawu, Piripati rrakiyangilawu
Kurukawangawakawayi
They are happy because they have speared the dugong

Wunijaka

Spirits of the wind

One of the women's most loved and regularly requested songs, 'Wunijaka', is sung for smoking ceremonies and healing in the lead up to funerals and Final ceremonies, when a loved one is ill or to raise the spirit of family and friends. 'Wunijaka' is sung at occasions outside the Tiwi community too, when the women wish to include their audience in communal healing, such as after the devasting bushfires in south-eastern Australia in 2020, and then again in the face of the global Covid pandemic.

Wunijaka means the wind, and, especially for people with Wunijaka Dreaming, the voices of their ancestors in the trees, singing and calling to heal. Wunijaka also means breath, as the breeze and the fresh air of Country enters our bodies and gives life and strength through our connection to the land. Some people also hear in these words a Catholic prayer to Our Father, and the Women's Group will sing 'Wunijaka' at Mass, with those same words filled with religious symbolism.

The songword Ngarrangarrangatawa is difficult to translate. 'Ngarra' means 'he' and also 'here is [something that has been found]'. It gives the sense of comfort and peace from the presence of an all-encompassing higher being – be that your God, your ancestors, your connection to the land or however it is that you understand and experience metaphysical love, harmony and spirituality. For singers and for listeners, the power of the words to soothe and heal is palpable.

'When we sing, we feel the spirits of the wind help our own spirit lift up. When we sing for people who are sad or when they are sick we feel a bit better and it makes us stronger to cope through sad times.'

Sheba Fernando

Wunijaka

Jipayamurriningimirri Ningingajima Pawunapi
    Yukujingima Yipijita
Ancestor names and places

Jipiyaputuwiya pirramanimpa
When he's up flying, rising up

Parriwingunji ngimpiya ngimpuniwunjiyalajirri
We keep telling each other this story

Ngarrangarrangatawa
He's up there, above, the most high

Yita warra ngawarringani ngirringani
Our great grandfather, our father

Pirripi kuriyuwu ngininginunji ngimpiya pirrukutuwiya
    pirramanimpa
They are up above and we stretch out our arms

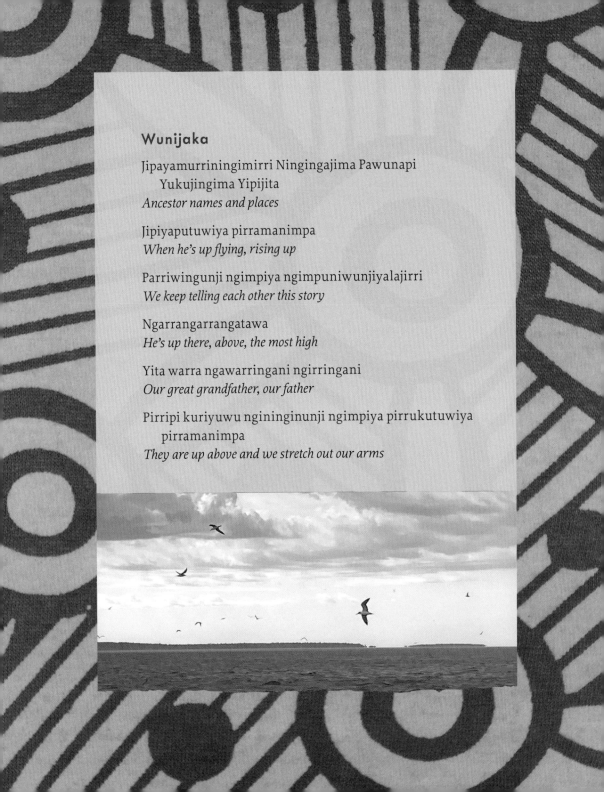

Ngirramini ngini karri Piripini Murntawarrapijimi

The song about a brave man who brought peace to the community

This song tells the story of Murntawarrapi, Emmanuel Puruntatameri, who stood up to call an end to the fighting between two local clan groups, the Jilarrruwi and the Takaringuwi. He saw those two families fighting and so he thought, 'I need to go in the middle to break it up'. Then he was struck by a throwing stick and he was killed. That made everyone feel bad and sorry that they were fighting, and it gave them shame and they made peace with each other.

Murntawarrapi's accidental death was seen as a sacrifice, and his bravery to stand up and call for peace shocked everybody enough to make them realise they must stop fighting and live as a community of Tiwi across all the areas of the islands. These spear-throwing 'mock fights' were not intended to end in death but were an important part of community politics. His death and the need to change some elements of clan politics is regarded as emblematic of the change in the Tiwi community regarding 'the old ways', and since then there have been no tribal fights of this kind. The song was first sung at Kulama in 1949 by Murntawarrapi's father, Pilayapijimi, to put the incident on public record. The story has continued to be told, carried along the Puruntatameri family songline. Clementine Puruntatameri (pictured, centre) passed on the words in this new version to her children, who sing it now.

The tune borrows the melody comes from a well-known song, 'Ten Guitars', written in 1967 by Gordon Mills (also known as Englebert Humperdinck). Tom Jones's cover of this song was popular in the Tiwi community in the 1970s. It's only the tune that we have borrowed for our song; all the words are completely different.

Ngirramini ngini karri Piripini Murntawarrapijimi

[Kulama introduction: Clementine Puruntatameri]
Ngintarangini nginiwatu wunturruwiyapirrukutuwiyapirramanimpa
People are looking at him flying

Parlingarri yurruma Jilarruwi amintiya yurruma Takaringuwi
Long time ago there was the Jabiru tribe and the Mullet tribe

Kiyi japinari Murntawarapijimi yiwatuwuriyi pinkaringini
In the very early morning, Murntawarapijimi went and told this story
Yuwurtiyarra ngawa-rringani ngiyatuwu tamarruwuriyi
He told his father, 'Take me, I will step forward'
Ngini wiyi ngiya-rringanuwi papuranjuwi wurima
He said, 'I will die so that they will all have peace, to stop fighting'

Yita Rangini ngini-watujurru-wiya-mpirra-marnipa
He has returned to his Country. At Rangini, people are looking at him flying
Pirripalukuwi pitini-wati-muntulu-wiya-lumonjigi
He is dancing up there across the sky
Ngiya pirratupu Yamparriparruwi yamurruntu
I am the great Yamparriparri [shooting star] and I'm so big
Yita Warriyuwu ngirrati-ngujurru-wiya-pirra-nginiliyi
Then he landed there in his homeland, Warriyuwu

Wutatuwu yurruma Jilarruwi pirratimirrikijiti minikawujinga
They the Jilarruwi stood up and hurled their throwing sticks
Awunuwanga yurruma Takaringuwi pirratimarrikijiti minikawujinga
The Takaringuwi picked up their weapons and spears
Waya awungarri pirratuwarri ngarra waya awungarri
And then they began to fight against each other
Murntawarapijimi purli yiwatiripi
And then Murntawarapijimi, standing in the middle, was speared

Ngarra awungarri Payakirrijimirri pwanki yiwatirimi
His father stood up and called for peace from both tribes
Nyilipajinginyawu minikawujinga pili waya ngiya-mirani
He told them to throw away all the weapons, it's over, my son was killed
Purliyiwatiripi kuwayi yiwatupumi ngarra-marrukulupi
And then he called out to both tribes to make them stand still and stop
Pirlimkiti pirratimimi wutamirani, wuta marrukuluwuni
Everyone sees their wrongdoing and all cry for their son and brother

Kurawu, awupi, ayi, kurrupuwu, ninja
[Jungle Fowl calls of the Puruntatameri lineage]

Milikapiti front beach

Ngirramini Ngini Ngarra Turimpi
The story of Turimpi

'My father, that's his father, his maningawu.
He was my great-great aminayi.' **Marcella Fernando**

This song tells the story of Turimpi Munkara, and was first sung by
Marcella, Olive, Glenda, Eucharia, Josie, Gregoriana, Greta, Della and
Apollonia in 1992. They called themselves the Top Enders, and they sang
it using a Jikilaruwu Country melody.

It is a complex song and holds far more meaning for family than its
translatable words suggest. In 1921, Turumpi (pictured above with Enrail
[left] and Antonio [right]) was an esteemed Elder and a patriarch of a lineage
that now takes one of his ceremonial names, Munkara, as a surname.

At this time, Catholic missionary Father Gsell, who came to be known
as the 'Bishop with a hundred and fifty wives', began trading with senior
Tiwi men to 'purchase' female babies and young girls for goods such as
flour, sugar and tobacco. This was to remove them from what he saw as
unacceptable – their traditional way life and marriage system – and baptise

them into the Catholic faith. He 'bought' the first girl in 1921, making this a difficult period for the inhabitants of the islands. The ideological conflict between the missionary and Tiwi culture must have created tension amongst families and clan groups, as senior men were disempowered, young girls and babies were placed in the mission dormitory, and the structures of traditional Tiwi society began to be dismantled.

The song describes Turimpi as a strong, dependable man who supported his family and followed the old, proper ways. He was proud and brave too, as he turned to face the white men to say, 'Pwanki' (peace). Not explicit in the text, but embedded in the associated knowledge passed down with the song, is that Turimpi was concerned at the questioning of the proper ways and cultural laws by people such as Father Gsell. He felt the shame of his loss of respect (in our culture way) from his family, and so he left his Country and went to Darwin to remove his face from perceived judgement around him.

In Darwin, he died of shock when he saw the headlights on a car for the first time, coming towards him out of the darkness. He thought they were a flash of lightning from the evil spirit, the Yamparriparri.

'He died while he was alive,' is the way Babui, his friend who was with him, described it.

We can't be sure, but the song records his sudden death as a heart attack from the sheer terror of being confronted with the evil spirit. Perhaps in his mind, it was a punishment for his failure to uphold tribal law and traditional culture. There are various stories about the Yamparriparri – the flying spirit – that are seen as bad omens associated with evil. It is either a warning or a response to bad things happening. An unexplained light low down in the sky, it is sometimes described as a shooting star, or a flash of light, or it is like the Min-min lights of other Australian culture stories. We can only imagine the terror Turimpi must have felt, never having seen car lights like that before. His death is remembered as a sad symbol of the old ways meeting the new.

Ngirramini Ngini Ngarra Turimpi

Parlingarri Turimpi yimuwu Jikilarruwu
Long time ago Turimpi lived at Jikilarruwu

Ngarra yuwutapirrani marntuwunyini amintiya jarrakalarni
He was so strong that he could catch dugong and turtle with his own hands

Ngini wuta ngarra-mamirampi purruwapikani
To provide for his children to eat

Awungarruwu kapi wuta tangarima yimamini
There where they camped

[Country places]
Manguntuwu, Kilimiraka, Yilinapi
Turtiyanguwu, Yawarlinga, Japarranapi, Tangiyawu, Ampuwanikiyiti,
Kukuni, Artawunapi, Wilipingirraga, Pawunapi,
Jawularimi, Pumpuruwu, Kirrilili tingata

Awungarruwu kapi Jawurlarimi tingata
There at Jawurlarimi beach

Awuta wurumurrunta purumuwu awungarruwu kapi ngarra
    murrakupuni
Those white people lived there in his Country

Ngarra waya ngini yuwuntakuwuna awinyirra walimani
They had an axe, so he ran away

Pirrimatakuwuna yuwuntakurluwunyi 'pwanki' yikimi
They chased him, he saw them and he stopped and turned around and said,
    'Pwanki' (peace)

Kunukuluwi pirima awuta ngarra-mamirampi
All his children are all grown up

Yuwuntakurluwunyi karri pirimarrimuwu awuta wuta-aminiyatuwi
He saw that his children were breaking tribal laws

Waya awungarri aliranga pirrikiyimi wuta-rringani
They made him feel ashamed

Waya awungarri yipirranyumwari Puwanikiyiti
So he left Puwanikiyiti to take that shame away

Ngarra yipatuwula Jiliyarti tingata
Then he went across to Jiliyarti [Darwin] beach

Yipakurluwunyi awarra yikwani yinimajirrakiningija
He saw the bright light [of the car headlights]. He thought it was flash of shooting
   fire, the Yamparriparri flying spirit

Waya awungarri yiminga yikiyakilimigi waya awungarri jimarrarami
Then he was so shocked that his heart stopped beating and he suddenly died

Pirlikiti yimimi yirikijika ngarra-rringani
They all cried in sadness for their father

[Ending...]
Ngarra awungarruwu yipirranyumwari
That's when he left
Puwankiyiti Pwanki!
Puwankiyiti Peace!

'This has given us a way to show our community, especially young people, that Tiwi singing can be maintained and developed using new ways of making music while keeping the old ways strong.' **Teresita Puruntatameri**

Tarntipi mangroves

Pangiyatuwi

Ancestor Song

Pangiyatuwi is an ancestor of the Portaminni line, a great-grandfather of the women who are Portaminni sisters. Rosemary, Jacinta, Frances, Augusta, Regina and Mel Sheba (above) tell the story of their grandfather aminayi, which was told to them by their mother and grandmother. Pangiyatuwi was one of the senior men who travelled across from Yeimpi, the eastern part of Melville Island (also called Sunrise). With other brothers he came to the lands along the southern coast of Bathurst Island, looking for women to marry and to establish new clans. He became the patriarch of the area of Makapurrumuwu, around Tarntipi, near the waterhole. He had five wives and many children. The Portaminni women composed this song to honour him and to record his story in song to teach their children an important lesson.

Along Tarntipi tingata (Tarntipi beach) is a tidal creek lined with mangroves that curves towards the east. The creek is safely traversable at

low tide but becomes dangerous as the tide comes in, so people must be careful and avoid walking there during the high tide. The death of this man in his Country while in the act of providing for his family has become a 'cautionary tale' for all his descendants. The women sing the song and teach their grandchildren about that creek when they go to Tarntipi.

There is also a moral to the story that the women tell in their speaking around the song. Pangiyatuwi is described as a man who knew his Country well and was a provider for his extended family. He took his family to Tarntipi, calling out to the ancestors to acknowledge respect and ensure a safe welcome into his land for himself and his family. He left his family in a safe spot, raised up from the water line and sheltered from the wind; it is the place where people sit today to make a fire and wait for those who are out hunting to return. The storytellers explain that Pangiyatuwi knew about the creek and the dangerous sands on the turn of the tide. He died because he went out a second time to collect more turtle eggs, as his children were not satisfied with what he had brought back. With this song, children are taught that they should be happy with what they have.

Pangiyatuwi

Ngawa mini yinimarruri ngarra purnayuwi amintiya ngarra
    mamurampi
He brought with him his wives and his children

Awungarra wuta tangarima ngampi murrakupuni
He called out to that Country place

Ngawa murka nginitawuluwu wuni ngawamini
We lost him a long time ago, our grandfather

Arikuta ngarra wantirrana pupuni
He was a very good man

Ngarra ngurri ngarri mini
We will never see him

Ngawarringanuwiwi purutumarti karaka
He collected eggs for all our fathers

Api yuwuntiarra muwa awungarra
He told them he would look around here

Augusta, Marie-Carmel and
Jacinta going hunting at Tarntipi

Api karri yipatuwala kurrukala
He went across the creek

Waya awungarruyipa mulujupa
He got lost forever in that place

Ngawatu makayimi ngawa yirriangarri
Where is our father? They said

Awuta ngawarringui pirripangirra
That is what they said, they were worried and wondering about him

Ngawuni ngawuni kulala ngawurrami
Let's go and look for him

Tinga tinga pirrimarri mapiyalupurri pirrimapiya kuluwunyi
They carried him up from the beach

Waya awungarru wuta pirikijika ngampi Wurrarikini Pirripingimamula
Then they buried him at Wurrarikini Pirripingimamula [sacred place]

Ngawangurri ngawa mini
We have never seen him

Jacinta

Mulankinya

The song about the arrival of the mission

The biggest change to the Tiwi's autonomy on their islands came in 1911 when Father Francis Xavier Gsell, a French priest of the Missionaries of the Sacred Heart, arrived to establish a Catholic mission on the south-eastern tip of Bathurst Island.

For this song, we tell the story of when Father Gsell came to the Tiwi Islands. Mulankinya and her husband Julanimawu were the first Tiwi people to meet him. We used the tune of the Christmas carol 'Oh Come All Ye Faithful', and we call Father Gsell 'Patakijiyali'. Old people heard his name, and in Tiwi when they said it his name became Patakijiyali.

St Therese Church, Wurrumiyanga

Mulankinya

Mulankinya, Julanimawu japuja yima Pipiyanyumili
*Mulankinya and [her husband] Julanimawu, they came from that
    Country Pipiyanyumili*

Piniwatipapirraya arnuka karrikuwapi purratuwunayi
There was no one around, no one saw them as they watched

Waya awungarri pirruwurtiyarrajirri
They asked one another who those strangers were

Muwa kuwani nginaki arimurrunta awujiingimuwu
'Who is that white man?' they said

Karri purruwunjingimuwani, awungarri yuwunuwayorri
They were sitting down and he [the white man] came up and asked them

Maka pirimanyimi awuta kapinaki arikurtumurnuwi?
Where are all the others of your people?

Wuta tangarima Jikilaruwu, Wurankuwu, Malawu, Munupi,
    Yayimpi amintiya Jamurlampi
They are all out in their Traditional Country homelands

Muwa kuwani naki arimurrunta wangimarri ngiya Patakijiyali
Who are these white men? He answered, my name is Father Gsell

Ngiya karrampi nginingunjirramarnipa
I have come from a long way away

Ngiya ngawa-rringani ngini waniyangirri
I was sent by God to come here to bring the message about the good news

Yinimintangirri awungarra Nguiu
He sent me here to Nguiu

Ngiya Patakijiyali nginimarruwariyi pupuni ngirramini
I am Father Gsell, I bring the good news

Apse decoration
inside St Therese Church
on Bathurst Island

Ngarra awungarri yuwunimajirrangirri angatawa yampatuka
He showed them his glasses

Pitipakurluwunyi wuta awungarri purruwurtiyarrajirri
They saw him and they told the others about him

'Ngawuniyi, ngawurrayakurluwunyi awarra arimurrunta ngini
ngarra karrampi yinipukularri'
*They told each other, 'Let's go and see him because he came from long,
long way'*

Najiwutawa arikurtumurnuwi punuwuni ngintanyimi
They came along all together for the first Mass [under the tree at the beach]

Pirripirranyumwari ngini wutawa murrakupuni awungarra
They all left their Country and came together

Nguiu japuja pirikirimi ngarra awungarri Patakijiyali mampara jurra
yikirimi
At our Country, Bathurst Island, a man named Patakijiyali made the first Mass

Ngini kama awinyirra naki Purrulipiyangiminga

The great big whale got stuck

'We sing this song about the time that whale got stuck in the creek, just around from front beach, near Myili Point, right here at Nguiu just past the barge landing. It was long time ago. I was still a schoolgirl. It was a huge whale. Her big round back was filling up the creek. Maybe she took a wrong turn because she swam up the strait and into the full creek thinking maybe she would take some shelter or find food. Maybe she was already tired. She was stuck there when the tide went out and so the men went down with their harpoons and speared her. Then everyone was happy because we had a good feed for the whole community. Everyone shared, down at the front beach.'

Jacinta Tipungwuti

There have been sightings of whales around the western and northern coasts of the islands, but only rarely. The story of a large whale coming in so close to the town is still an extraordinary tale, hard to believe except when told by those oldest men and women who saw it with their own eyes. The huge feast enjoyed by everyone is an important part of the retelling. It was by chance that the whale beached itself in the creek right next to town, which meant that its body became a gift of nourishment to the community rather than going to waste.

Murli la

Ngini kama awinyirra naki Purrulipiyangiminga

Kurrukangawakawayi kawayi kawayi yikawayi
Kurrukangawakawayi kawayi kawayi yikawayi

Mintatingapi tangarima juwaringunjikirimi
It was at Mintatingapi, a whale came from a long way out, from another Country

Angiyi Mintatingapi nyirra tangarima juwaringunjikirimi
At that place in the creek at Mintatingapi she made a home

Nyirra arnuka tuwanga awungarruwu nyirra yimatirranyuwiya
'I will never go back, I will stay here,' she said to herself

Karri waya mangilipwani yiwatuwujirrapipirraya juwarimani juwari-
ngunjingumurupiyangiwamiya
*Then the tide began to go out and she tried to move around, to turn around, to get
out, but she couldn't. She was stuck in the shallows*

Japi japinari pirratuwujingi-marriwayoriyi
*The next morning came, when people went down to the shore, wondering what
was going on*

Ngini ngajingawula awungarri ngintingikitarriji
They all got a fright

Ngini ngajingawula ngiti-murriji-ngini-ngitanyimi ngini kama awinyirra
naki purrulipiyanikiminga
*They all gathered around together to have a look and she was the biggest whale
they had ever seen*

Kukuni, kukunari ngintiwati-ngujingi-marrawurrimi
gini ngajingawula waya ngimpatiwunjingapa
They all were happy and full up after eating that whale

Jipurrupuwu

Wunijaka
Cyclone Tracy

The story goes that just before the cyclone was approaching, on the afternoon of 24 December 1974, an old lady came up to people, shaking the leaves in her hands and yelling, 'Yita wurra wunijaka ampungani kupnganiyai!' ('The wind is about to come and destroy our land!'). When we perform this song, someone will call out first like that old lady.

The cyclone moved almost all the way around the Tiwi Islands, from the north-east, across the top and down the western side, then turned south-east and crossed the far south-western tip of Bathurst Island, with 120 kilometre per hour winds recorded at Cape Fourcroy. A lot of trees came down in the storm but there was comparatively little damage on the islands, as the cyclone headed straight to the mainland. It hit Darwin and destroyed 80 per cent of the houses there and killed seventy-one people.

The melody of this song is borrowed from 'Mississipi', a song played on the radio in the mid-1970s, performed by the Dutch group Pussy Cat. Old ladies Apollonia and Victoriana, who knew the old language, gave us the hard words for this song.

'When we first began composing these songs back then, it was important for us that the old language was kept alive in our new songs, and the words we learned from our Elders were put in alongside new ways of saying things.'

Mary Elizbeth Moreen

Wunijaka

Yita waya yati walimani pakitiringa yuwuriyi
That day in the pakitiringa season the cyclone came after seven days of the rain

Karri waya awungarri pirikuwaniyangirri
They radioed across. They sent messages, contacting each other

Ngini awarra ngirramini purruwangirri ngini waya awinyirra wunijaka
   ampinganikipirnami
They sent the message, story about that big wind coming and is going to hit us

Ngarra nguriyi Jiliyarti nginingawula tangarima ngawa ninganuwanga
   ngimpinganipingintayi ngajingatawa
Timani ampingimi ngarra nguriyi murrakupuni
*We feel sorry for Darwin, we won't forget about all the land, all the places, all the
   suburbs that were destroyed*

Purimarriwayaningimarri awarra ngirramini niyi maka arrami
   wutatuwu
Arramikuta, arramikuta, awunga wuta waya
Awungarri yiminga yuwuntakilimigi
All the people huddled together. They were all in fright and shock
After the cyclone they all went together for help
They had broken hearts for everyone hurt from that cyclone

Marruwau

Nginingaji ngatawa murrakupuni ampingimi karri
All the Countries [suburbs] were affected

Piripirtangaya awarra ngirramini awuta alawuruwi
The big bosses tried to work it out, decide what to do

Purruwuniyangirri angi wutawa purruwunani awinyirra wurra
All the big planes had to stop flying

Purruwuntakupalamigi kangi wuta murrakupuni
They all went back to their own Country – [the Arnhem Land, Tiwi Islands,
    Port Keats mobs who had been in the city]

Wurumurrunta amintiya ngawa turnuwiyi wuta
Arnuka kukunari pirimi pili awuta wuta mamanta
Yintuwu purruwuntimwariyi
All the white people and us mob were all the same, all together as friends
    being unhappy because they lost their families and houses

Purrukuparli by Owen Tipiloura

Japarra, Purrukuparli amintiya Wayai

The ancestral story about mortality

This song was created for a Mother's Club Eisteddfod performance, led by Clementine Puruntatameri. The tune is a sunrise melody, said to have come from the birdsong at dawn and taught to the Traditional Owners of Yeimpi Country, the land over which the sun always rises.

   Purrukuparli was the son of Murntankala, the old lady who created the islands. This is the Tiwi story of Purrukuparli, his wife Bima (also called Wayai) and their baby son Jirnani.

   It tells how baby Jirnani's death brought death to the world for the first time, and then Purrukuparli held the first Pukumani ceremony for his dead son. Purrukuparli's brother Japarra became the moon, establishing the cycle of night and day and of the tides, and we still see the scars from that fight on his face. Bima became Wayai, the Bush Stone Curlew. Wayai walks around at night, crying – crying for her baby son and her husband and her lover who died because of her.

Japarra, Purrukuparli amintiya Wayai

Japarra, Purrukuparli amintiya Wayai japuja yima Yayimpi
Japarra, his brother Purrukupali and Wayai, they lived at Yayimpi

Kiyi Purrukuparli yipurrartiyi ngarrmirani, Jirnani
Then [Purrukuparli and Wayai] made a son, Jirnani

Kiyi Wayai juwartirimi ngampi nyirra-purnayi Purrukuparli
Then Wayai wanted to go hunting, but Purrukuparli was there waiting for her

'Nginja awungarra tangarima tayamangi nginja mirani'
'I want you to stay and look after our son here at our camp' (he said to her)

'Pili ngiya watuwuja wajaka jiwatipumiyangirri' Wayayi
'But I want to go walkabout,' said Wayayi

Ngarratuwu yintuwu yunuwatirima juwujinguntapirri
He came behind her, looking for her

Kiyi Purrukuparli, kuwayi, kuwayi yimarruwayuwuriyi
Then Purrukuparli wanted to humbug her, argue with her, because she had left their son

Ngarra purnayinga nginja-mwarti arnuka
He called out to her but she didn't answer

Yurrupujiyarringa nyirra-purnayi
Her boyfriend (Japarra) blocked her mouth

Wayayi, Wayayi, Wayayi pili ngiya tinga tiya Japarra yimi ngampi ngarra-yuwuni
He called out, 'It's me, I'm Wayai'
Japarra answered, (still pretending to be Wayai)

Nguntaluwapa muwa-mirani ngiya yiminga ngimpitirripiliga
'Give me our son, that little boy, I'll bring him back to life'

Yimarrimapiyuwuliyi, Purrukuparli yimarrimapiyuwuliyi awarra ngarra-mirani
He grabbed that little boy, he wanted to take him, he grabbed his son

Wayai by John Babui

Purrukuparli, Japarra, pirrimarrimapiriwarri
Purrukuparli and Japarra argued and fought
Wuta-mirani Purrukuparli juwunga murrukuwunga juwuniyani
They had a fight with fighting sticks, Purrukuparli threw it and hit his brother
Japarra juwunga mujurrukuruka Purrukuparli yuwuntunupa
Japarra threw a stick too but Purrukuparli ducked his head and it missed him
Japarra, kiyi tiwirriyi yuwuturmi yiwalayapurti kuriyuwu
Japarra, then, he went up to the sky

Yimarrimapiyanginili ngarra-mirani yimarrimapiyuwuruwamani
Purrukuparli stayed with his son
Yimarrimapiyanginili ngarra-mirani tingatinga yimarrimapi
    jipulimanyimagi,
He went down to the beach, he walked carrying his son
Ngawulayapunyanyimi yimarrimapingartigi ngarra-mirani
'We've all got to follow him, my son, he died, we've all got to die'

Japarra

Yinjula

The old lady

This song begins with the old lady (performed by the most senior woman present) talking and muttering to herself as though in a state of confusion, before the song-proper begins. It is acted out in a humorous style of self-mockery, with the old lady and her feebleness gently made fun of. 'Yinjula' is symbolic of the oldest woman in the traditional extended family unit. She can no longer contribute to the group's daily responsibilities but must be loved and cared for as the Elder. In our

performance, as the others sing about her, Yinjula will wobble and sway, leaning heavily on a walking stick, acting out the story of being lost in the bush. As well, she usually acts as being blind, confused and disoriented, but she's safely tied by a rope so she doesn't wander off. She continues to 'groan' and 'yawn', 'ayayi' as the others sing.

'Yinjula' is also sometimes performed at the end of traditional ceremonies, with similar words sung in classical form, and the old lady role can be equally well danced by a senior man. The text in this version includes many words from the old language as well as alterations to become songwords. Leonie Tipiloura, pictured here dancing Yinjula, is the current star performer of the old lady role for the Strong Women's Group.

Yinjula

[The old lady talking]
Ayayi! Niyi kama warlani amunujingipirni?
Ayayi! Why am I yawning so much?
Ayayi, pili ngiya waya nguwuja, api maka ngiya marnutumwani
    amintiya tirtikiya
I'm heading off walking now, and I need my walking stick

Ayayi...

[The song]
Jipajirringi Yinjulagayi ampinuwi ngurrupa ngalagayi
The old lady kept on walking with her stick

Jipartirti tirtika ampiniwingila pirtiyagayi
*But still she keeps on walking around leaning on her stick [and groaning about
    being tired]*

Marntulumwarni jinnikunjilajirringijipwarawurrukimiya
She tied a vine rope from the bush around her waist so she won't get lost

Jipartirti tirtika ampiniwingilapirtiyagayi
And still she keeps on walking

Ngingaji kuwinari jinnipwanjirringalamulumanagi
She becomes very old, her skin, her face all turned into wrinkles

Jipartirti tirtika ampiniwingilapirtiyagayi
And still she keeps on walking

Kurrukangawakawayi Kurrukangawakawayi

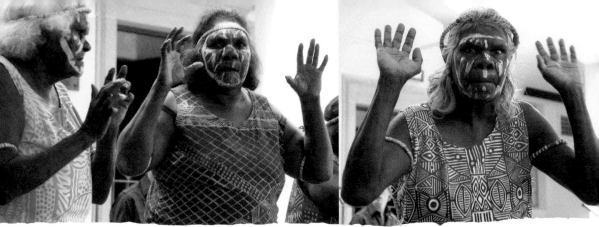

Leonie, Teresita and Jacinta dancing Nyingawi

Nyingawi

The people who hide in the bush

The Nyingawi are small, hairy people who live in the bush on the islands. They are the people who were here in the Dreaming times, before Tiwi, and it was the Nyingawi that taught Tiwi people how to hold Kulama. It is believed that there are still some left and they go about their lives hunting and camping in small family groups deep in the bush and singing and speaking in their own language. People sometimes say that the small fires that start in the bush for no reason might be from their campfires.

People say they still see them occasionally, out of the corner of their eye, or they sense the Nyingawi watching from behind the trees. If disturbed, they usually run away and hide, but sometimes it is said they will sneak up and grab someone if that person strays too far alone in the bush, especially at night.

Nyingawi is an ancient songline, held through the past century by members of the Munkara family and danced by people with Nyingawi Yoi. It includes some words sung by Munkara (recorded in 1928), his son Enrail Munkara (recorded in 1954) and Enrail's son Stanley Munkara (recorded in 1975). When the women perform their modern version, the

most senior singer with Munkara or Nyingawi lineage will perform the Kulama words. Some of these words are not translatable but have been passed down through the years, intact because they are in the Nyingawi language and so they never change. The Women's Group composed this storytelling song to sing to their grandchildren to warn them not to stay out after dark and not to venture into the bush alone. They dance as the Nyingawi, sometimes holding leafy branches in their hands to 'hide behind' and with actions that resemble scratching and pulling at their hair as if they're bothered by lice and fleas.

The repeating strain, in the Nyingawi language, ends with a grunt '*a-mm*'. As they make this sound, the women in their dancing move towards their audience with outstretched hands as if to say, '*Boo!*' Their little grandchildren shriek with terrified delight. This is another example of how we continue the traditions of Tiwi song through re-invention and responding to the contemporary aural environment. The old Nyingawi words, with their metre and syllabic count intact, are reworked seamlessly into the tune of Cliff Richard's 1972 hit 'Sing a Song of Freedom'.

Nyingawi

[Kulama words]
Jipangalapirrikutawurra amm, Murtati yuwunjirranamila amm
Nginja awungarri kirama nyimpiripirnijarra m,mm
Jipangalapirrikutawurrana, Jipangalapirrikutawurra m, mm

Ngampi Yuwulupi yawurlama wuta awungarruwu Nyingawi purumuwu
There in the jungle they the Nyingawi live there
Wuta yingwampa purruwuriyi Tumarripi, Tiritiringa, Tuwartipi,
    Pirnimawu, Punjilawu, Yimarlanu
The others lived in those places [Country places]
Wuta waya awungarruwu tangarima awujingima amm
They will always live there

Wuta pakinya Nyingawi pitirikipirni ngirawiyaka
They were the first people singing in the Kulama
Waya awungarri pirimi [Murru-jayampi-jingilaja]
That's when they said [Nyingawi language]
Yita murruka ngintuwujingimarripurtuwa
Then hurried back to where their children were
Pawuraji-yuwujingi-majingi purruwu-jingi-rramiya m m
Juwujikimiliyani purru-wuni-majingi-purrukuwuna
[Pitirijikilamwari] wuta Nyingawi pirimi
[Nyingawi language] those Nyingawi said
'Ngawulimpwari, ngawulimpwari'
'Go away, go away'
Wuta Tiwi purruwunipirni wuta waya awungarri pirimi
The Tiwi hit them then they said
'Wurruka, wurruka amm'
[Nyingawi language (in pain/scratching themselves)]

Wuta waya awungarri Nyingawi pirimangarti
They were there, the Nyingawi drowned themselves
Wuta Tiwi pirripakupawurli ngampi wuta murrakupuni
Then the Tiwi went back to their Country
Waya awungarri Tiwi pirimi
Then there the Tiwi said

Kurukangawakawayi, ngampikangawakawayi, kurruk amm

Wurruka amm!

Darwin Festival, 2017

Arawanakiri by Bede Tungutalum

Tini Ngini Yirrikapayi
Yima Kapi Wiyapurali

The Crocodile Man

Kimarriyanginila is a word found in very old songs. Made up of Old Tiwi spoken words, it means 'strong tail' and 'a lot of', or 'an intensity' of something. It is no longer spoken, but it has become a songword to refer specifically to the Yirrikapayi ancestor, the Crocodile Man, now called Kimarriyanginila.

The Arawanikiri is a heavy ceremonial spear, with long barbs carved down both edges of the spearhead, and on the most elaborate, along both ends. Its broad shape resembles the tail of Yirrikapayi, the ancestral Crocodile Man, who was the first to make this type of spear and who, as the songs tell us, was chased into the sea to become a crocodile.

Tini Ngini Yirrikapayi Yima Kapi Wiyapurali

Kurrukangawawayi kawayi kawayi kawayi

Kimarriyanginila arawunikiri ngarra yuwunjirritirramuwani
The Crocodile Man is sitting down making a spear

Kapi ngawata tangarima Wiyapurali tingata
He was at his Country/home Wiyapurali on the beach

Ngarra mamanta Jikilawula pirrimiwangirlinjiga
His people [of the tribe] Jikilawula did not like him

Pilimurrakupuni ngarra yimajirranyuwiwurliyi
Because he did not share the land

Pirlamirrawu jingimuwu pirlamirrawu jingimuwu
Lying low down in the mud

Turliyuwurtimi awungarri yimajurtungimarnuwa
When he crawled away and he changed into the crocodile

Waya ngampi mirripaka yimajurtiyapingari wu
He crawled towards the sea with the spear in his back

Wiyapurali yu wunjingimirrapi yamurrijingi kipijimi
At Wiyapurali they saw him – he was running very fast

Wiliya arawunikiri jingirrawamiyakilimigi
The sharp pointed spear went through its back

Pikilijipiyanginila winga winga ampakulumurri
Crocodile goes out with the sea

Ngarra-mamanta Jikilawula purruwurtiyapamula
His people [of the tribe] Jikilawula did not like him

Nginjatuwu waya awarra nanki nginja Yirrikapayi wuwu!
They all said you will be, from now on, the crocodile wuwu!

Jikilarruwu

Jikilarruwu Country Song

The words of this song are held and passed down by Jikilarruwu People. Jikilarruwu Country stretches across the southern part of Bathurst Island, and the chorus section names all the special murrakupuni places as you walk through them in turn. You follow the places marked with sacred sites and features that are considered family, because they are the places where all Jikilarruwu People find their spirit and where they will go to after this life. There are very old grave sites and ceremony poles in these places, some so old they have long fallen over, but they are left undisturbed. When the women go into their Country, they call out the names of loved ones and ancestors who have returned here. These place names are part of that calling out, acknowledging and saying hello to the inlets, shoreline, the creeks, waterholes, ochre cliffs and the long coastline. These places are so imbued with the spirits of the ancestors that they are family.

The place names and acknowledgement of Country are more important than the melody, and so they completely override the rhythmic patterns of this new melody, borrowed from 'Happy to be on an Island in the Sun' by Demis Roussos. That song became part of the Tiwi environment from the late 1970s. Listening to it made the people think of their island in the sun and that led to them composing their own song. The old ladies still listen to it through their grandchildren's phones and often sing their own words along with Roussos's lyrics.

Jikilarruwu

Ngawa nginingawula murrakupuni Jikilarruwu
Our Country Jikilarruwu

Wuta ngawa-ampi awungarruwu tangarima yimamini
Them our grandparents, long ago they used to live there

Ngawatuwu awunganuwanga ngawa nginingawula murrakupuni
    Jikilarruwu
It is also our place, our Country Jikilarruwu

Ngawa kukunari ngimpirimi nginingawula timani
We are all happy in our Country
We are naming Murrakupuni places in Jikilarruwu, in order that you would walk

Mawuntuwu, Kilimaraka, Yilinapi, Turtiyanguwu,
Places along the coast [where you get white ochre clay]

Yawarlinga, Japarrinapi, Tangiyawu Ampwanikiyiti,
Along the coast right up to where the lighthouse stands

Kukuni, Atawunampi, Wulipingirraga, Pawunapi
Places inland, and near the fresh water, the creek and then at the other side

Jipirriyapa, Pirnimata, Malikuruwu, Jawularimi
Places after Pawunapi going north along the coast

Ngumpupuji jupunyini amintiya Kilimpiti
Looking from the cliff at Kilimpiti

Yurruma Murntanimpila

Stone Clan

This song was composed by women of the Murntanimpila, Mullet (also called Takaringa), which symbolises the water and includes a clan of Jilarruwi (Brolga people) as the Brolga fishes in the shallow waters of their Country. It is one of the women's culture songs, helping children of Mullet and Brolga groups to identify with their maternal Country, totems and songlines. When they come together to hold ceremony, the Jilarruwi call out and hear the ancestors in their Country. When Jilarruwi dance Brolga at ceremony, they are Brolga, manifesting that ancestral being in their actions, and that Dreaming-time ancestor dances through them, straight from Country.

The image of the Mullet people being caught in the net is not a sad one. Instead, it signifies the collecting of the mullet for nourishment and the continuing cycle of the life-sustaining connection with the environment. It is also a metaphysical cultural bloodline, creating a bond between the people and their ancestral Country, now embodied in them. The melody is a traditional tune from Malawu Country, sung by Eustace Tipiloura in the Kulama way for Brolga People. He shared it with the women for their songs.

Yurruma Murntanimpila

Ngawa-yurruma murntanimpila ngawa ngirringanuwi agayi
Nginta ngawa pirratimani ngunjirraningimarramigiyi
Ngawa ngirringanuwi watimani ngunjilani kitimigiyi pili ngawa
Luruwantuwi watimaningunji ngimamula
Mantakurupayinga wuta pirratipingipirranginikirimi
Ngina-mingawa naka awungarra yoyi ngimpatuwunjingimi
Nginta wurlujungala pukwiyi kuwayi jiwatuwujingimi
Ngawa-yrruma Jiarruwi ngimpatu wunjiliyarrajirri
Nginta ngawa jilati awungarra nigmpatu wunjingi kiringirri
Jipapularri ngawatu wunjurru punjinga kiringirrapa
Ngawa yurruma takaringuwi ngimpatuwunjiliyarra jirri
     pungupurti mirripaka
Ngintiwatuwunjingimangili yamanyirra pungupurti mirripaka
Ngintiwatuwunjurrwantiyapukulupiya
Nginta wuta panapa purrunjirri kimajingingimpirrapingari
     kurrukawanga wakawayi
Ngayurruma murntanimpila nginta wuta panapa purrunjirrikimaji ngimpi

*We are the Stone clan group and we gather together on our sacred
     ceremony ground*
*We hear our fathers saying that we belong to them, telling us that
     we are important*
We make the ceremony ground clear, ready for dancing
We are all dancing together now
We call out our Dreaming, calling out from Country
Jilati dance comes in, through us from that Country
The group comes in to dance Jabiru Jilati
Dancing like that Jabiru with wings going up and down
*We are now the Mullet people, swimming, jumping and flipping
     in the sea, singing now we are there in the water*
We get caught there by the net, they throw out to catch us
We have our bloodline from that Mullet clan, Mullet Country

Ochre on
mussel shells by
Doreen Tipiloura and
Jacinta Tipungwuti

Ngariwanajirri

The Strong Kids Song

This song was made over some months in 2011, in a project funded by the Northern Territory Red Cross Communities for Children program. The Strong Women's Group spent time with their grandchildren in several sessions singing, dancing, telling stories and teaching them some of the old words used in songs. The children were encouraged to think about phrases, mottos and 'rules for a good life' to contribute to the lyrics, which their grandmothers then composed into songwords. All the lyrics came from the children's requests and favourite words.

We created four different versions of 'The Strong Kids Song', by each group of children, aged between five and seventeen, and set them to melodies from each community. This setting of the words brings all those groups together. The song begins with a traditional call out to Country from Clementine. It then incorporates melodies from Munupi and Mantiyupi from Cynthia and Rosemary (pictured overleaf), as well as a modern spoken section performed by the high-school students.

Ngariwanajirri means 'We all come together' or 'We all work together to make good things happen'.

Ngariwanajirri

Kurukangawakawayi kawayikawayi kawayi

Karri ngumpuriyi kapi ngawa murrakupuni
When we enter our Country we can feel their spirit calling us

Ngini wutawa walima api ngawa kuwayi ngumpurumi
Make proper law to live well

Kapi ngawa ampi ngini yinukuni ngarimuwu
That our ancestors have done for a long time

Najingawula Tiwi ngawayati ponki ngarrimi
To share, to keep our peace and remember

Ngariwanajirri ngawurra ninguru magi awarra ngini
Ngariwanajirri working together to listen and helping one another

Ngawa ampi ngamaninguwi putuwurumpura Tiwi ngirramini ngini
    ngawa ngampangiraga
Hang on to old stories from our ancestors that they left behind

Kurukangawakawayi kawayikawayi kawayi

Ngajirti awa jawayamulinjupa
Let us not lose our culture and the language we speak

Ngawatu kapinganki kakarrijuwi ngawurraningirrumarri nginingawula
    ngirramini
We young people get together

Ngawurra ngungurrumagi ngini ngawa ampi ngirramini
    putuwurrumpurra
We remember our ancestors' stories, passing on from generation to generation

Ngawa ngawutimarti kakarrijuwi ngini pupuwi pumatama
We want our children to be strong and healthy – to follow the right path

Ngawurra ngingurrumangi amintiya kukunari ngawurami
We support one another and are happy and to be a strong people

Pilingawa yati ngaparinga ngingingawula pupuni ngirramini
We are the Tiwi that speak our Tiwi language

Ngawa-Manginguwi Ngawa-ampi Karri Karluwu Jana Yuwunipirnani

Our grandmothers and grandfathers lived in Country

The Strong Women's Group often take their grandchildren out bush, showing them the places to collect bush foods and telling them about the flowers and shrubs that are useful, or that should be avoided. They point out the many endemic plants that produce edible fruits, such as the Yankumwani (*Buchanania obovate*, green plum) or Piniyama (*Syzygium suborbiculare*, pink beach apple), and explain in which season they can be eaten. The women know the best places in the bush to seek out 'sugarbag', the native bee's honey, and teach the kids how to prise open the exposed roots of mangroves at low tide to pull out yiriwuli (mangrove worm). They show them how to boil the leaves of Murinyini (*Acacia oncinocarpa*) to make a medicinal treatment for chest infections, and to collect the leaves of Jikiringini (*Alphitonia excelsa*) to crush with water to create a soapy lather.

The bush foods are so good for our health and in the past the old people had less sickness; they were healthy and strong, and they felt comfortable in their land, sharing what it provided for generations. These days, with too many people just eating junk food and relying on the shop, we hope young people might be proud of their grandparents and start to follow those ways again. The natural environment has so much nourishing food to offer us.

This is one of the songs we composed to teach children about their history and culture, and to tell them how important it is to know about the bush and how to hunt and collect bush food. It is passed around singers of the Munupi group and we use a melody from that Traditional Country.

Murli la

Marralayingimpi

Ngawa-Manginguwi Ngawa-ampi
Karri Karluwu Jana Yuwunipirnani

Kurrukangawakawayi, ngampikangawakawayi
Kurrukangawakawayi, kawayi, kawayi pirripangurlimayani warta,
    murrakupuni
Ngawa-ampi, ngawa-maninguwi
Our grandfathers, grandparents
Walked a long way through the bush in Country
Awungarruwu piniwungamini wartiyanginila
That's where they got bush food
Api wuta awarra purruwapikani
They ate bush food

Jipwajirringa, wuninga, yilinga, jarranga,
Wallaby, possum, carpet snake, buffalo,
Wurrikiliki, milipukani, wakijapa, arrayi, muputi,
Goose, mangrove worm, bitter mangrove worm, oyster, fish,
jarrakalarni, marntuwunyini, wurlanga
turtle, dugong, crab
Api awarra, arnuka jana yinuwuntapirnani
And so they had no sickness

Arikuwakitori (mango)   Catching wurlanga (mud crab)

Waya nginani ngawapa ngini wuta wurumurrunta yinkiti
Now today eating white people food
Ngini yingarti minaya tamulanjini
With too much fat and sugar
Api awarra jana amunimajingipirni
Makes us sick

Ngawurrangurlimayi ngawurramirnangili
We all walk together, come together
Api ngajiti ngawujamuwu awungarruwunga
And don't forget the ways
Nginingaji ngawa-ampi pirimamini amintiya ngawa-manginuwi
Like our grandfathers did in the past
And great-grandfathers

Marralayingimpi Creek   Jarrakalani (turtle)

Wurnatawi

Wurnatawi Song

These words are like those in kinship songs we sing for ceremony. Each song adds to the voices that seep into the bush and come back into us when we go there, or when we sing these words. The Warntarringuwi, the Sun clan group people, are one group who call this our homeland. This song was composed by Warntarringa women using a melody from that place, to show their pride for their clan group. When they sing the last phrase, they dance as the current Custodians of the land and the current dancers and singers and tellers of the ancestral stories.

Walamajarra

Warntarringa (sun) floor mat
by Calista Kantilla

Wurnatawi

Ngawa-ngimani wurnatawi atawi nginti-
   wari-ngilimpa-ngimajurru-mamu
We are the Wurnatawi People

Ngawa-yuwuni payawurra nginti-wari-ngilimpa-ngimajurrurrumamu
We belong to the land of around those places along the shore and in the bush

Kangi jarrumawunga ngawa ngintini-ngunji-ngimaju -wuntu-
   wumamani
The songs carry their sons and daughters through the Country

Naka awungarra wurrumiyanga ngintiningunjingimaju
   wuntumiringarriji
We are all here now together at that place where those cycads grow

Warntarringuwi wuta waya awungarra wuta pirratuwinjirra ningimarri
The sun clan group all come together in this place that is ours

Ngawa-ngimiraninga naka awungarra yoyi watimirrringunjingimi
We are all dancing for our people and our children

Warntarringuwi jilatinga ampikimajingikirrayunjirramirratingami
*The sun clan group dances on the ceremony ground, holding the ancestors
   inside their bodies*

Payawurra

Payawurra Song

This story has been handed down through Wurangku singers for longer than people can remember. On a literal, physical level, it tells us about a man who is approached, while sitting on the shoreline in his Country, and told that his daughter has passed away. On a metaphysical level, it is an enacting of the return to Wurangku, Payawurra Country, and to the ancestral spirit world that the deceased are processing through. The women sing it at funerals or at a Yiloti (Final ceremony).

Within the song the 'voice' shifts from the current singer/s telling the story (with the old man in the third person) to the man himself, who voices the action through the last five lines. He sings Crocodile Dreaming in the story, then calls the others to join in. Those last five lines can be heard as the old man singing in mourning, or in the voice of the current performers who sing in his voice. When he/they sing 'Come together to sing', it is a direction for all those present to join in mourning, as well as from the old man to those he was surrounded by back then, and from all the ancestors along the lines of the Payawurra People's deep past, back to the ancestral Crocodile. 'We all come together to sing [for funeral when a

sister dies].' The singers – the women and the old man – then sing that Yoi, which they've called people to take part in.

The penultimate line is an embodiment of the action, of the singer/s, of the deceased and of the ancestor. The women say that this is not the man singing those words, it is them describing what he (and they) are doing as they dance. The words we can translate in these final two lines are 'winga' (sea), 'ampakulumurri '(to go out like a fire), 'nguji-' (a long way away), '-ampi' (ancestors), '-wala' (the spirit of a dead person) and 'riyi' (to go, to leave). The words are understood to give the sense of a departure to another place. Pikilijipiyanginila has become the name of the Crocodile ancestor. The final line sings about the old man, his deceased daughter, the woman being sung for now, and all those with Payawurra Crocodile Dreaming when they take the journey of the deceased.

Pajuwapura

Payawurra

Ampurruwayiyi niji ngarra wunji ngumuwani kapi ngatawa tangarima
   Payawurra tingata awi
The old man was living there at Wurangku on the coast at Payawurra

Jurrukupulayu nyirra jiwatuwunji nigmarruwari kapi nyirra rinngani
   awungaji jiwatingunjinginayijiwati ngunjiliyarra nginja waya
   wurnataga jiwatiyi-ngunji-ngimiya
*Jurrukupulayu found him there sitting on the beach. She had to find him for sad
   news, to tell him that he had lost his daughter*

Angatawa yiminga ngarra yiwatu-wunjirran-kilimigi pirlinkiti
   awungarri yiwatu-wunjingi-majingi-papurti
He was shocked and he cried and called out and he began to dance in mourning

Mangirriwayi ngarra pakinya yiwatiyi-ngunji-ngiwanga yiwati-ngunji-
   ngiminta
He sang for grieving and for his lost daughter [Crocodile Dreaming for her]

Pikilijipiyanginila winga winga ampakulumurri
Crocodile ancestor swims out to the sea

Payawurruruwula wuta pirratu-wunjingi-waya-kinajirri pili pirratu-
   wunji-ngimi
All the Payawurrura clan came together in groups to sing

Pikilijipiyanginila yungujiliyampi-ngima-yawalari
He danced Crocodile actions for Dreaming

Pikilijipiyanginila winga winga ampakulumurri kurrukanga wakawayi
He dances Crocodile, swimming out to sea, like that ancestor singing
swims out to the sea
disappears out to sea
fades away [out of sight]

Yirrikapayi (crocodile), fabric
design by Vicky Agnes Portaminni;
ironwood Tawatunga (sticks)
artist unknown

Ngimpirimajipwapa karri Ngawa Ngimpiriwayatipi

The effects of drinking

Traditionally sung by the Muluwurri group, when this song is performed by the women they choose one or two to act as the drunk people, swaying and tripping and swigging their imaginary beer, trying to dance Yoi and mock-fighting. It is always a funny, light-hearted song to perform, and the older ladies especially ham up their acting to poke fun, even though the underlying message is a serious one. They are well aware of the problems of alcohol abuse and its impact on First Nations communities especially, and don't shy away from it. There is also understandable frustration at the way the problem has become a generalisation for Aboriginal and Torres Strait Islander Peoples, with misunderstandings and preconceived notions that often lead to unfair and destructive outcomes.

Although this song was created to speak to the Tiwi community, we want people to understand how alcohol can be fun and enjoyable but too much can be damaging to you and to those around you – no matter who you are or where you live. In Tiwi we say, 'Kangi wuta punyipunyi amintiya mikajanga' – a little like in English, 'In one ear and out the other', as the drunk person doesn't listen or think carefully about what they hear.

Accusing a Tiwi person of having no name and not knowing how to dance, as we hear in the song lyrics, are strong insults. Names are bestowed at birth and through life at important milestones and for achievement. Having no Tiwi name implies you have no place, no respect and no standing in the community. Not knowing how to dance (one's Yoi) is unthinkable. It is one's identity and personality. The drunkard throwing these abuses here paints a picture of how they don't know what they're saying. Some of the old ladies do enjoy a beer and happily admit to getting a little merry with a drink in hand. That's okay, they say. Everything in moderation.

Ngimpirimajipwapa karri Ngawa Ngimpiriwayatipi

Kapi wuta wurumangampa awinyirra mankirrika
Those who drink alcohol
Nyirra wiyi awungarra ampirimanguwayangiraga
It makes them talk too much, say things you wouldn't normally say
Kangi wuta punyipunyi amintiya mikajanga
In their head and out through their ears
Wuta awungarri wurumajupwapa wuta-amiya
They start fights, they think they are better than anyone

Mana tipami jajiruwi, kuwulingimpi,
They start calling out, disrespect, 'You got no Tiwi name'
Minangijajiruwi, ngiya ngilawa
'You don't know how to dance.' 'I'm the best, I'm more top than you'
They're feeling tough

Kurruwukangawakwayi, kurruwukangawakwayi kawayi, kawayi

Wutatuwu kapi wuta yartipwarri mamirnikuwi
Those mob who are sober, they are the ladies
Karri wuta wupaminangili pakitarrini
The ladies, they're gathering 'round playing cards
Karri wuta-mwaruwi kirirra wungajirri
When the kids are teasing, scrabbling
Wuta awungarri wurumajupwapa wuta-mwaruwi
The mothers say, 'Don't hit my child because that just makes you look bad.'
Then everybody starts arguing

'We change the length of each line of the tune so it suits our Tiwi words. The melody gets stretched out across the words. We don't try to squeeze in the words to the tune, it's the Tiwi words that are most important so that tune gets shaped a bit to fit. The words are as important as the melody, the meaning of the songs.' Eunice Orsto

Ngarramini ngini Pukumani

The song about Pukumani ceremonies

Maggie and Dulcie Kelantumama composed the original words for this song. Translated here by Rachel Kerinaiua, Gregoriana Parker and Augusta Punguatji, it was a difficult song to put into English. While it involves relatively few words, the song holds rich information about the correct and proper ways of observing mourning protocols (called Pukumani) by the pirrimaruwi (the old men and women, the ancestors).

It incorporates old hard words and phrases that don't translate completely into English or into New Tiwi. The women who composed it knew the old song words and we are lucky to have them written into this song for us to learn and to pass on. Some of the text is in translation and the words in brackets give a description of what is happening in the song, which is itself a description of the procedures followed in the old traditions of Pukumani. At the time, the embedded information was presumed to be known by all, and words that held associated meanings were more complex than direct translation can provide. Attempting to translate it now, there are words that even the oldest singers don't fully understand and can only give suggestions for.

More than just the ceremony itself, it tells how the next-of-kin is in a state of restrictions during the period of mourning – not walking about, not holding food or drink, painting and repainting face and body designs and wearing ceremonial armbands and headdress for an extended time. It explains the mamanunkuni sorrow singing and marks the restriction on speaking the deceased person's name. This is a very important piece of cultural record.

'Old people when they were Pukumani, that's what they used to wear, long time. This song comes from old ladies. They sang this song long time – because they remember their ancestors, great-great ancestors, our great ancestors. From them to us.'

Concepta Orsto

Preparations for Pukumani ceremony near Milikapiti, photographed by Axel Poignant, 1948

Ngarramini ngini Pukumani

Ngawa ampu ngawa maninguwi karri wunata pirimani
Our ancestors' grandfathers, grandmothers, when they've lost their loved ones
Awungarri pirimajawatuwani
They are all sitting down
Yarirringa, pamijini, palipalini
Using red ochre, painted up all in red, armbands, men use them

Ngarra nguwuriyi pukumani miyuwiyaga
He's not allowed to touch food, to hold food, give him tea, he's Pukumani

Pipingimaji wapunganu pungurragayuwujirriki pirramatuki piyawurligi
Karri jiniwatikirrijimani awungarri
They sing when they cry, in that way of being Pukumani
Pirratimajingipaputiyamini mamanikuni purratuwayamukurigani
Dancing and singing mamanunkuni, for sorrow, to show respect
Pili awarra warntirrana yirrikamini
Really true, you don't say the name

Yiloti (final) grieving in Pukumani ceremony.
Yirrikapayi (crocodile) Dance in the Pukumani ceremony, Bathurst Island, photographed by Charles Hart, 1928

Karri waya yinkitayi piriminangani pirripangimarrani kangi
    yirrapumuni
Yoyi pirimani ngini piriwangamini kujungura
    purimarrikuwangipayamini
[When they're ready they are all coming to the Final ceremony
That's when they wear the special ornaments, feathers, armbands and painted up
    for their clan groups. They come together for dancing and singing.]

Waya arrulupuni makatingari pirimani
Awungarri pirikiripirrayamini pirrimarrikuwantiyakupunaliyagani
Awungarri pirrimarrikuwangipipayami
[It was the ending of the ceremony, makatingari, when they wash off the ochre
    colours and that washes off the sorrow time. It's like a cleansing. They wash
    away the cover-up disguise that was protecting them. That person's soul has
    departed now. Gone to their Country.
Finishing off ceremony, here is how it happens.]

Pukumani ceremony.

Turtuni poles for Pukumani ceremony,
Melville Island, photographed by Axel
Poignant, 1948

Tiwi Nginingawula Ngirramini

It is good news that the Tiwi land is ours

This is one of the songs composed after the Australian Government policy changes of the 1970s, which acknowledged First Nations land rights and resulted in Tiwi people regaining some control over their Traditionally-owned Country. The young women, whose husbands were on the newly formed Tiwi Land Council, were emerging with pride in their Tiwi identity and wanted to put on record their sovereignty on the islands. The subject matter of these songs saw a subtle shift from the historical songs telling of the arrival of the missionaries and of the benefits of the farms and buildings, to songs reclaiming the land itself and re-affirming precolonial Custodianship and heritage. Naming the Countries echoes the calling out of Countries in ceremony, which serves as acknowledgement and respect for ancestral lands and ancestors. It also claims those lands for the current Custodians and adds their voices to the songlines that wind around the islands through the songs and ceremonies that have come before them.

Tiwi Nginingawula Ngirramini

Parlingarri, wuta ngawa-ampi purumuwu kapi warta tingata
   murrakupuni Jikilaruwu, Wurankuwu, Munupi, Malawu amintiya
   Jamulampi
Long time ago our ancestors were here on the beach, the land, their Country …
   [all the Countries]

Ngajiti ngawajangiliparra ngini wuta ngawa-ampi ngirramini
We never forget our people all come from our great-great ancestors
Awarra ngawurraningurumagi Tiwi nginingawula ngirramini
We Tiwi people keep our culture and our stories strong

Awuta nga-ampi amintiya ngawa-maninguwi wuta karrikamini
   purruwuni
Our ancestors, our grandfathers and our grandmothers didn't have much,
   but only their culture
Parlingarri waya juwa ngini kularlaga pirimani yinkiti
Long time ago they only had what they found, they hunted bush food
Purukuruwalamini Kulama Yoi pirimani
Kulama and ceremony were very important in those days

Wuta nguriyi ngawa-ampi, ngawa-maninguwi awarra pupuni ngirramini
We thank all our ancestors for our strong, good culture and stories

Putuwupura ngini yoyi ngarimi amintiya kurlama amintiya ngini
   jilamara pirikirimani
They left us our culture – Yoi, dance, Kulama yam ceremony and [body and face]
   painting design that are very important for Tiwi people

Ngawa-mwaruwi amintiya ngawa-mamirampi ngawa-ngilipi
Our parents and our relations, our great-great ancestors

Ngawa-mampi ngawuntajipiliga pili ngini awarra wupaliyipirri
   ngirramini
Our long-past great ancestors have shown us and taught us to keep our culture
   strong

Yiloga

The Football Song

The melody in this song is considered a derivation of the melodies from Paru, from the south-western shore of Melville Island, in Mantiyupi Country. The tune is known these days as the 'happy' tune that was sung by old women when they went out bush, so they could keep in contact with each other and not get lost. The ladies also use it for many of their 'topical' songs in community events, because it provides an easily recognised melody as the basis for new words to tell the story of a relevant current event. So it is quite easy for people to join in, even with the changing lyrics.

The Strong Women's Group sings at the Tiwi Islands Grand Final every year. Their renditions in Tiwi and in English of the Australian national anthem and 'The Football Song' are firm crowd favourites. Although the song stays almost the same each year – telling the story of a football game and describing the important elements – small changes are made to reflect the teams that are playing and the Country they are affiliated with, and to acknowledge visitors from the mainland and important guests who might be in attendance. The words and photos here are from the Grand Final game between the Imalu Tigers and the Muluwurri Magpies, on 7 May 2022.

Yiloga

Najingawula Tiwi mamurruntawi ngaripinguji ngimajakulumu
All of us, Tiwi people and white people, are watching the game

Imuluwula Muluwurrila wuta kali winguti ngi marruwungilupi
The Imulu and Muluwurri teams are running into the field with the ball

Ampayamani yilowaji wunjingimpiya mantuwuni
The umpire with the football bouncing the ball

Wijilipayamanangirri pulamuningayurugi
*[Descriptive of the umpire's action bringing the knee up and arms down
  to indicate a goal]*

Wurrukurrunuwi wujingimarri piningijirri ngajirrami
Young people are pulling each other's football jumpers

Kuruwamuta wutawungaji wíngumjingímpi nawajirri
Punching, pushing, tackling one another

Jipakawularumagha ampijipiningintagayi
He gets a free kick and he kicks a goal

Najingawula yajilotuwi kukunari ngaripingujingimarrimi
Every one of us [Australians] are really happy to see the best team win

Nirrawaya awungarra yilowa ampijingi piningimpaya
That's the end of the football season 'til next year

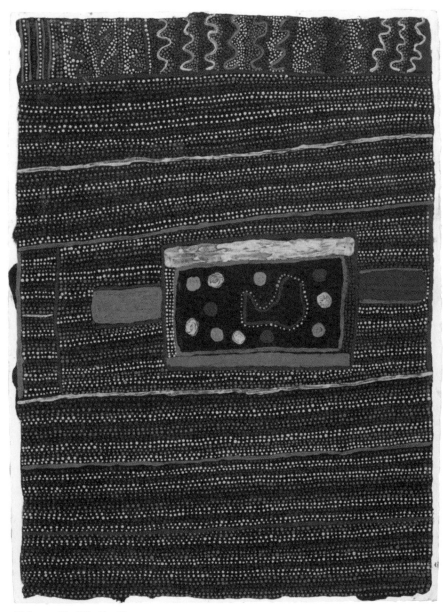

'Pukumani' by Kitty Kantilla

Kumurrupuni Yikwani Ampiliwanikimutamini

Smoking fire dance actions

This song is sung for the Mamurampi, the sons and daughters of the deceased. Each line describes the dance action performed at the Yilaniya, the smoking ceremony held the evening before a funeral and before the Yiloti (Final ceremony) by members of the family to mark their relationship to the deceased person. The songs and the dances performed at smoking rituals represent kinship through symbolism known by all Tiwi people. This song was composed by the women to bring some of the songs and dances used in smoking rituals together in a teaching song for school-aged children.

First it refers to those with patrilineal kinship who dance together as 'daughters' or 'sons'. They dance holding their hands near their groins to symbolise their father. Next are 'cousin-siblings', who dance placing their hands on their cheeks or the side of the face; an injury to their face described in a song symbolises their pain, being in mourning. Those women and men who share kinship with the deceased's mother will dance as mothers. Their loss is symbolised by a gesture in which one holds one's middle as if feeling the pains of labour. Then the matrilineal siblings dance with injured or hurting legs to mark their relationship and their pain, in grief. The amparruwu, the widow, dances with a hurt shoulder, weighed down by the burden of mourning, which she bears on behalf of everybody as the closest kin to the deceased, the spouse.

The dance, which imitates holding up spears, allows people to express their anger at the death, symbolically wanting to fight the situation and find something to blame. Embodying kinship and enacting anger and pain is a cathartic process that, through the dances and the songs, lets people grieve with others around them in safe and supported ways.

Kumurrupuni Yikwani Ampiliwanikimutamini

Wanga ngawa ngirrininganuwi
We, us, our fathers

Nginta ngawa tokwayinga
We hold the tokwayinga [goose feather ball]

Pirrimanu-ngujirra-muli
They belong to us, it's ours the ceremony ground

Ngawa-mamanta
Our friends, fathers, nephews, children in the patrilineal bloodline group
Ngawa awungarri ngawampi pangiyaringa pirrima-nungujirramuli
We are on the ceremony ground

[*Sung for the Wurnatawi: the group who represent the father of the deceased, son or daughter*]

Ngimpala
Son- or daughter-in-law
Palampalini ngumpurrukujiwili wamurnukutirri
We wear that palampalini [white cockatoo feather headdress]

Yamarringa purlinga juwingirrawuli
Both hands held on top of leg at the groin

[Mujini: *Cousin–brother or cousin–sister*]
Arramikamini yiminingirri kurupumuli piyarlingi
Something slapped me on the side of my face

[Wurnataka]
Mother who has lost a child
Nginja parnaparti awurriyawi
You are the mother who had a baby girl or boy
[*Dancer is holding around her middle like in labour pain*]

Yirranikara
Brother and sisters, mother's side
Jipanikiripi yanikiripi janagayi
Clapping hands on thighs, aching leg

Amparruwu
Widow/widower

Nginji yupurrini arintiya
Apalamaya nyimparimayakini
Timirrikimaka arluka luka ngumpurru-kujiwilingi-mayakini
*[Fighting sticks used in mock fights for ceremony. The dance is arms
  raised above head, like holding sticks]*

Yiloti
Ngawa awungarra ngamirri-ngunjurru pujingaya mirratigi
Everyone takes part for final dance to close the ceremony

Art Gallery of New South Wales, 2008

Nginingawula Yinkiti

Bush foods

'It's about collecting mussels, women collect mussels and mangrove worm and piranga, and men, they go looking for possum, kangaroo, geese, dugong and go hunting turtle.'

Regina Kantilla

This is a simple song for children to learn the Tiwi names for the main bush foods on the islands. The inclusion of ngilinya is important. It is the cycad palm nut. When eaten raw these nuts make people very sick and can be fatal. They are, however, a rich source of nourishment in traditional gathering practice. Understanding how to deal with them is essential for people's safety. This song is especially important for those who don't know much about the natural bush foods. First roast the nuts in coals, then crack them open, peel the shell off and grind the nut to a crumble. This is then soaked in water for three days and nights. It creates a good flour-like dough for making bread. We sing a Milikapiti tune and women from there are the holders of the song.

Jukwaringa (mud mussels)

Murputi (fish)

Nginingawula Yinkiti

Ngawa Tuwurrampila tangarima arima awungarra lakatinampi
    murrakupuni
We are Tiwi people living here in our Tiwi Country
Ngarra ngawa-rringani yinkiti yimuntakirayi kangi warta amintiya
    kangi mirripaka
Our fathers gave us good healthy bush tucker from the land and the sea

Arrayi, muputi, kuluwarringa, jarrakalarni, marntuwunyini, yirrikapayi
Oyster, fish, mud mussel, turtle, mangrove worm, dugong, crocodile

jipwarjirringa, wuninga, marinyi, yilinga,
Wallaby, possum, bandicoot, carpet snake,
Yingwati, ngilinya, wurrikiliki
Sugarbag, cycad nuts, magpie goose

Ngawa-rringani ngarra ngawa yimantamuwurli kapi nginingawula
    yartirrikani
Our ancestors have given us this knowledge to pass on

Jampulampi, Jikilarruwu, Wurankuwu, Malawu,
Lakatinampi awungarra ngawa tangarima
[Countries] our land

Kurrukangawakawayi, ngampikanga wakawayi

Yankumwani (green plum)

Piniyama (pink beach apple)

Aya Ngirringani

Healing Song

This beautiful song is for healing, for remembrance and for prayer. The song provides singers and listeners with healing, as the women sing to both the Holy Father and the ancestors to ease the pain of sickness, when singing for a loved one who is ill, or for the end of suffering when near death. It is also sung to lift the weight of grief and sadness after a death, prior to funerals and other mortuary ceremonies, and at any time in remembrance for passed loved ones.

Recording Aya Ngirringani in the Old Church on Bathurst Island

Aya Ngirringani

Kurrukangawakawayi, kawayi, kawayi

Aya ngirringani ngintinirimarruriyi, jirti yilipiga kangawa purnikapa
Oh, father, we have sickness and bad feeling inside us
Awanga ngamatama, yatari ngimpirimajigi,
We are struggling with this
Nguntawani ngawa ngirringani
Help us our father

Kurrukangawakawayi, Kurrukangawakawayi, kawayi
Kurrukangawakawayi kawayi, kawayi

Ngirringani nginja yati nyimpurumungurumi ngini ngawa
    naki jirti ngirramini
Father, we know you, you know everything that is bad inside us, sad thoughts

Tawunawu awarra jirti kangawula ruwuti ngawatuwu nguntapuluga
    ngirringani
Throw away the bad feelings in everybody, comfort us

Aya ngirringani ngawa nginja ngirringani
Oh father, my father
Ngimpingiyipungintayi kangawa punyipunyi
We know you, we think of you in our thoughts [also refering to deceased loved ones]
Ngawatuwu nguntawani, Aya Ngirringani pili nginja warntirrana
    nginjila Ngirringani
You are the most highest power I look up to you

Tiwi+Jazz performance, University of Sydney, 2019

Nginingawula Ngawa-ampi puturupura

Our ancestors, they left those stories for us

The chorus of 'Nginingawula Ngawa-ampi puturupura' lists the woven and feathered ceremonial regalia used in the past. In the Palingarri (the deep past), birds were the dancers and the ceremony holders and their feathers still carry great significance for cultural practice today. In the past, senior men leading ceremony wore full feather beards (the feathers were collected when dropped from passing black cockatoos, or when hunting magpie goose), string and possum-fur necklets decorated with feathers, and elaborate headdresses, mostly made of the feathers of Yinkaka or Pipingilirri, the sulphur-crested cockatoo.

There is a sense that when this song was composed in the 1980s, it was regarded as a song about heritage. The verses tell of Pukumani and include text that would have been sung by men in the traditional ceremony and Kulama. They name the ornaments they used and the ochre paints around their body. The melody is borrowed from 'Walk Away Let's Forget', recorded for Columbia Records in 1965 by Australian singer Brian Young.

From Munupi to Malawu

Nginingawula Ngawa-ampi puturupura

Ngarramini nginingawula ngawa-ampi
This is a story about our ancestors
Ngawa-maninguwi putuwurrapura
Our grandparents pass on their knowledge
Tangini purruwuniyangirrajirrani kapi turrampila
Tangarima yitumujingima
Message sticks take the stories around to family in their Country
Pipingilirri, yintiyintinga, pupukunyawu
Yarringa amintiya pamijini
[All the ornaments worn during ceremony]
Wuta awarra pukumani purruwunani awuta ngawa-ampi ngawa-maninguwi
That's what our ancestors wore for Pukumani, the dressing for ceremony

Jajirrima wumunga kurlama pitikiripirnani
Three days men have Kulama ceremony
Purrumirrikuwamilani, pirrimirrikiyaningamini
When they sing, when they gather together
Ayipa jupwakiyayi wuta pirratirimani
When sing the end [Ayipa] it's the end of Kulama

Wuta nguwuri ngawa-ampi ngawarringanuwi
Amintiya ngawa-maninguwi api ngawa ngumpunuwungujingipingintayi api
Thinking about our father, grandmother, thinking about them, we still
*   think about that person*
Awarra ngawurraningurumagi
Let's hold on to it, that feeling, of who they are

Kurrunjakayi

Japanese Bombing of Darwin Song

This song tells the story of the Japanese planes that flew over the islands on their way to bomb Darwin in 1942. It was the largest attack on Australian soil during the Second World War, and we can still see the wreckage of a crashed plane at Pawunapi. The people on the islands, having seen the planes flying overheard and hearing the explosions in distant Darwin, would certainly have been talking about such a major and traumatic event.

Around March, early in the dry season when Kulama was held, was soon after the bombing on 19 February. The attack was put on public

record by singing about it in Ayipa, the third day of the Kulama ceremonies held across the islands that year.

When the planes strafed the islands (without causing injuries on the ground), Father Pat McGrath at the Bathurst Island mission radioed authorities in Darwin to warn of an imminent attack. As the story goes, his warning was not heeded. If it had been, the resulting casualties and destruction might have been avoided.

What has come to be known as the 'Japanese Bombing of Darwin Song' has continued to be performed on anniversaries of the attack and in public performances since the 1940s. Dance and actions play out the story, as dancers take the roles of the war planes circling in the air, as well as miming the actions of Pat McGrath, of the people on the ground looking skyward through binoculars, and of the ground-based gunners who eventually shot the planes down. The women take on the danced roles in their version, just as the men do in the Kulama ceremony version.

'Bombing of Darwin' by Pauletta Kerinaiua

Kurrunjakayi

Yita karri awungarri Kurrunjakayi piniwatu-wumajiki-pirralumuriyi
This is about when the Japanese came, when they were flying

Jirrangantuka, yangarntuka piniwatu-wujingi-kipirnamani
They had guns, they were coming with guns

Api wuta waya awungarri turrungampila pirratu-wujingi-kitarriji,
    pi wuta waya awungarri pirratu-wujingi-makipjimi
*Then when they arrived all the Tiwi people were afraid and ran into the
    mangroves to hide*

Waya awungarra ngawa-rringani yiwaturupinguji-waniyangirri
He radioed Darwin, telling them that the Japanese planes are arriving
Wuta manuka awungarri kuwa pirrimi-ngunjirri-pujingami
That they are on their way to the mainland, heading across, so take cover

Yita awungaji Julurupi pirratu-wujingi-kipinyawu
'They're flying over there'
Nginingaji ngatawa timani yati-yiwatu-pirrangu-lanikuwa
The Japanese turned around, coming back

Api waya awungarri kurrunjakayi pirratu-wujingi-nguwali-miya-kupawurli
Flying around they had finished, then they went back home

Murli la

A love song

Francis Orsto is a young man with exceptional talent in Tiwi language, composition and vocal skills. He learned this song from his amawu, Carmeline Puanjiloura, in the 1990s and then sang his own words in 2012. The melody is loosely based on a song by Bill Anderson, 'Once a Day', which is also a love song about missing someone and wishing you were with them.

Francis (pictured below with Leonie and Sheba) has been playing guitar for the Women's Group since he was a young boy. He often plays guitar and sings with the old ladies in performance and recording projects and has travelled with them around Australia. Although 'Murli la' is a women's song, the old ladies are proud and pleased that this rendition of their favourite is performed by Francis as lead vocalist and holder of the story.

Murli la

Karri nginta ngiya ngimpingingta kurruwuni
When you look at me

Ngiya tu awungarri kukunari ngirrimiji
That's when I'm happy for you/because of you

Apiwaya angilawayimingampulapa
That's when my heart starts beating

Murli murli la. Murli murli la.
Let's go, let's be together

Kapi ngimparrimi muwiyati awarruwu
Wherever you go that's where I will go too

Ngiya nuka nginta ngimpangintamurri
I'll never forget you, goodbye indeed between us

Ngiya ninganguwanga nginta ngiminipingitayi
That's when I think of you/am in love with you

Karri ngiya nguwarrimatirripi
When I'm sleeping

Yinilinjilayi manka ngimpangilingimi
An image of you comes to me

Api wayu ngarri yatari ngirrimiji
I'm looking around for you

Pilikama ngangi muwawangintajirri
Why are we apart?

Pupukatinga Mijuwalinga

Beautiful woman

This song is a fairly close cover of the song of the same name by Toots and The Maytals, from their *Knock Out!* album, released in 1981. The Tiwi version was created for a performance by the Muluwurri group in the local eisteddfod. The lyrics are newly invented in Tiwi, and tell a story about losing and missing a beautiful woman. It was best known as Tony Pilakui's hit song in the community, and in recent years it became a signature tune for Cynthia Portaminni (pictured here), a talented singer and musician and central member of the younger emerging singers of the Strong Women's Group. She was a lead vocalist, guitarist and keyboard player. When she passed away suddenly, she left a rich legacy of musical and performance talent. Our recording of 'Pupukatinga Mijuwalinga' is performed by Cynthia.

Pupukatinga Mijuwalinga

Maka arrami jiyimi anginaki tinga karluwu
Where's this girl, I can't see her
Ngamataya-kurluwunyijarra waya arrami jipamulijipa
    yiloti kangi yoni murrakupuni
Where can I see her, I'll never see her again, has she disappeared,
    gone to another place

Pupukatinga mijuwalinga nyirra nguriyi nguriyi agayi
Beautiful woman you are gone, I miss her very much

Pilikama awungani jipami ngini nyirra arnuka nimpangi?
Why did she go and not say goodbye?
Jimiturrumunangimi arramikuta nyirra arnuka ampirtimarti
I think it's because she doesn't want me anymore
Ngiya nyirra nguriyi nyirra nguriyi agayi
I miss her, I feel sad about her

Ngiya arnuka ngintimatangiliparra awinyirra
I will never forget her
Ngiya nyirra nguriyi ngiya
    nguriyi agayi
Oh, I will never forget her

Tiwi Papunuwurri

Shooting Star people

Clementine passed this song to her daughters Ella and Francillia, along their matrilineal clan. They dance Papunuwurri, Yamparriparri, the ancestor who came as the shooting star across the sky, also known as the Min-min lights.

> *'The words and the melody come from the great-great ancestors –*
> *music coming from all around, Papunuwurri he shared it around,*
> *we all now sing that tune from them.*
> *Mum, she listened to her people. They made up the tune themselves,*
> *the melody came from somewhere in the middle of Malawu.'*

Ella Puruntatameri

Tiwi Papunuwurri

Awi mamanta nyulipwaripa pili waya!
Pangirayinga, Pirratimani ngujirramuwurlu ngini yoyi
    ngimpatuwujingimi
[Calling out] Hey, everyone here!
All you Country people, we are all together here at the ceremony ground

Ngiyapurru-ngilipangiparrani natuwala milimika
We are all going to dance together at the ceremony dance ground
Kuwapi pimangitimi ngilipangi pirra ngini-yari-ngina ngawa
    Papunuwurri yoi?
Who will be the first to dance the Papunuwurri [Min-min light]?

Ngimpatuwujingimi mana nyilpayakiriparri nana awarra mana awarra
    yoi nyilipami
Let us all clap together and start dancing

Jipani tami tiyu wula kurti yami tiyu wula nginti ngawa kitipapuranjuwi
Dress yourself with the ceremonial armbands

Wuta Jurrampila pirratirimi nginta wanuwa kitipauranjuwi ngimpiri
    kitimyingali kukunari
All of the Tiwi tribes, you are the best dancers and it makes you happy and proud

Ngimpi ngani ngunji ngimarra kuwangimi, ngini wuta ngawa-ampi
They all say that you dance so well, like our great-great ancestors

Ngiya-mantanga arramukuta nyirra ampi ngini pungintayi
They all said she dances like a strong woman

Ngarra Awarra Ngawa-Rringani Yipangiraga

Love your neighbour

This is a hymn that we sing in church. The words were composed by Inez Tipungwuti and Daniel Paujimi, some of the men who were part of the crossover of musical styles as we added guitar and choral harmonies to our singing. As well as singing for ceremonies and passing on their knowledge of hard language and the traditional melodies, they also sang for church services in the 1970s. Since then, we have always sung in our Tiwi language for church services and today we sometimes sing hymns in English, but usually in Tiwi.

Ngarra Awarra Ngawa-Rringani Yipangiraga

Kurrakanga-wakawayi, kurrakanga-wakawayi

Ngawa ngajiti ngawulamiya ngawari-pingintayamiya
We don't only think about yourself, think about others

Ngarra awarra ngawa-rringani ngarra awarra yipangiraga
Our father tells us to love our neighbour

Kurrakanga-wakawayi, Kurrakanga-wakawayi

Ngawa ngijiti jirti ngawari-maja kunjingi-muwajirri
We must not forget, think about others
Nuwa ngajiti jirti myimpari-maja kunjingi-muwajirri
Don't hate others, love one another

Kurrakanga-wakawayi, kurrakanga-wakawayi

Kapinayi ngawa-mantawi ngampiripi ngarrangurupunya
We think about our friends and we think about our families

Kurrakanga-wakawayi, kurrakanga-wakawayi

Karri ngawuni pupuni muwunukini kirrijajirri nyirraluwajirri
Share what we have and share with one another

Kurrakanga-wakawayi, kurrakanga-wakawayi

Wangimarri awarra ngawa puranji ngawa-muwajirri
Love each other, love your neighbour

Warntirrana yipangiraga ngarra awarra juwungupira
God spoke to the people, love each other

Kurrakanga-wakawayi, kurrakanga-wakawayi

Murli la

Ngarramini ngini Jipuwunganarrukamirri

The story of the old man Robert Tipungwuti

Jipuwunganarrukamirri, Robert Tipungwuti, was born around 1938. He was a man of the Wurangku Country clan and of the Ironwood clan. This song tells how he decided to go back to his Country and take his family with him, rather than stay in the town where the government wanted them to be.

From 1910 to 1973, Tiwi people were under government rule, with the government deciding where they could live, who they could marry and where they could travel.

This song is considered an important piece of Tiwi political history as it puts on record the stance Robert Tipungwuti took in proclaiming his right to live on his own Country. The song was composed in the early 1970s. It includes some words inherited through the Nyingawi Yoi lineage. When we sing in the voice of the old man himself we sing, 'Jipingalampirrikitawurra ... wurrika, wurrika', words that he would have sung as he proclaimed himself by his Dreaming identity. The melody is heard in Wurangku Country and owned by the Wurangkuwula group.

Ngarramini ngini Jipuwunganarrukamirri

Jipingalampirrikitawurra ayikimajingipurruwumami,
   Jipuwarnarrikamirri yimuwu Mantarrinkuwu
Robert Tipungwuti lived at Mantarrinkuwu [Milikapiti]

Muluwuri yuwutiyarra ngarra-mwarti, tuwariyi kapi ngininginjila
   murrakupuni
That old man Muluwuri told his nephew, we should go to your Country Wurangku

Yipirranyu muwarrii awungarruwu Mantarrinkuwu
He left that place Mantarrinkuwu

Jipingalampirrikitawurra ayikimajingipurruwumami wurrika, wurrika,
   ayikimajingipurruwumami
[He sings his song] I am Jipingalampirri

Yuwuntiyarra Malawula Wurangkuwula
The Malawu and Wurangku People all come together

Wuta awungarri purruwutiyarrajirri 'Ngawulipuwariyi awungarruwu
   Timinipi'
They talked together about it 'Let's go to that place Timinipi'

Wuta awungarri kukunari pirrimimi yipirranyuwunyayi awungarruwu
   Timinipi
They were happy now that they were at Timinipi

Ngarra awungarri pinkaringini yikirimi, yuwunuwayorri
   kirrakunukuluwi 'Ngiyatwuwu ngintawani mamanta?'
*He wrote a letter to the government, he sent it to the big boss and he asked,
   'Please can you help me?'*

Jipingalampirrikitawurra ayikimajingipurruwumami
Wurrika, wurrika, ayikimajingipurruwumami
Murntatiyuwunjirrinamirla ayikimajingipurruwumami

[He sang his song]

Yipuwarnarrikamirri ngarra awarra Wurangkuwunila
The man from Wurangku

Wurrika, wurrika, m, m, m

Jukwarringa (mud mussels) by Lorna Kantilla

Ngarra miraninga taringa juwirri

His daughter was bitten by a poisonous snake

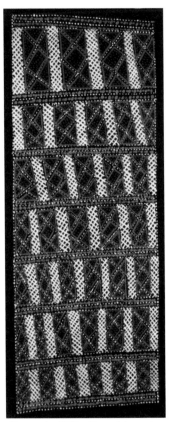

Jilamara by Shirley Puruntatameri

This might seem like a simple story about a girl who was bitten by a snake, but it is actually a deeply symbolic mourning song that follows old traditions. The song begins in the voice of the deceased young woman, who is in the state in between the living and the dead. She doesn't know what has happened to her, but she senses something is wrong. She knows that her father will look after her. She refers to him as Arlingurimirri, the ancestral Dog, her paternal Dreaming. These words also mean that all her ancestors will look after her in death. The women then sing about her – that she has returned in death to her Country. Next, they sing in her father's voice, as he calls people together to hold her mortuary ceremony in her traditional Country. Once that ceremony is held, she can move on to her next existence as one of the Mapurtiti. Here the women follow Tiwi tradition by voicing an ancestral spirit, evoking and acknowledging the ancestor and his connection to the deceased to protect her journey to the afterlife.

Ngarra miraninga taringa juwirri

Ngiya awarra ngirimajilamini ngirringaniya ngiya
I think that something has happened to me
Arlingurimirri aminijingi kuwaluwamami aya ngirringani
My father, my dog, will look after me

Wurriyanginapi murrakupuni ngarra-miraninga
Our daughter is there in that Country Wurriyanginapi
Taringa jiwurri api ngarra mangintalani mamanikuni
She was bitten by a poisonous snake – her father sings in sorrow, for worrying
Waya awungarri yuwayamukurigi, waya awungarri jiyimi
Then he says ... telling how she said

'Ngiya awarra ngirimajilamini
'Something will happen, what will happen to me'
Ngirringaniya ngiya arlingurimini aminijingi, kuwaluwamami aya
    ngirringani'
'It was my fault, my mistake being frightened and nervous'

Kawangawanikayayi kayayi

Aminijingi kuwaluwamami marrakitijimawu Purruwuntawulimi
    juwatimirri ngujurruwu
[He is saying to her sisters how they must mourn]
'Lingirrangiraga, Muntuluwu murrakupuni walimani ...
'That place called Muntuluwu Country
Purruwunimajatirrangirri awungarri mangintalini
That is where the ceremony will be held
Yingimani ngiya Wanamajuwa ngiwatuwu
[He is saying] I am Wanamajuwa [Reno Kantilla]
Jurrumunangimami yirritituwu purmali nguwatuwuja'
*I am going back to my homeland where we were once upon a time, where we
    originally came from, before we moved to Malawu Country.'*

Kawangawanikayayi kayayi

Tambuwu

The man who escaped

This song tells a long-ago story of the time when the British built Fort Dundas on the north-western side of Melville Island. Tambuwu was captured and held prisoner in a deep pit for some time. No one knows exactly how long, but oral stories and songs tell of how he grew thin from starvation. Nevertheless, his escape showed just how strong he was. He climbed out, reached Bathurst Island by canoe and went to Wurangku to raise the alarm. The song picks up his story once he was free – the part where he narrates the story of his escape to the others. People say that he wouldn't sing about his long, lonely days down the deep pit because that had passed and he was not that man anymore. The Munupi group created these words and melody and continue telling his story.

Lucinda, Bella, Shirley, Marie Simplicia and Michaeline at Pirlingimpi front beach

Tambuwu

Tambuwu ngarra awarra Wurankuwunila yinipirranyumwari
   Wurangku
Tambuwu, the old man, was living his life there at Wurangku

Yinipirranyuwunga awungarruwu Wajijapi, Wajijapi yipirrakurluwunyi
   timani
He then went walking and arrived at another place Wajijapi
Wiyawunga jinikiyanyuwumiji mamurrintawi pirikimajirramirna,
   api pirikimajinga awinyirra wiyawunga amintiya awarra
   arikurtumurnini
He got a raft and saw white people, and then went to near where they were camped

Tambuwu ngarra wiyi awungarri yuwunikijiyarra awuta Munupula
He told the Munupula people what he had seen
Nginta wanga ngurruwuntakuluwunyi awukayi nginta wuta marruwi
I saw mothers and children there

Yikiyamarnipa yikiwangulimayi awungarruwu kangi waya Pwangilaga
He walked across to that place, the creek at Pwangilaga

Ngarra wiyi mwarliki yuwjakumwayi waya kangi mirripaka
   yikiyakupurnali
And then he swam down that creek to the sea and he saw them
Mamurrintawi kularlaga pirranikima arnuka ninganuwanga
   pirrikinyayi
The white people were looking for him, but they never found him
Api wuta awungarri pirrarikantirramirna
They even shone a torch looking for him in the dark

Ngampi waya arrimuwu yikantirrapurti wartinga murrakupuni
   yikiyimamani
Then that old man kept walking and came along through the bush

Api yuwunikinyayi awuta Munupula awungarruwu kapi waya kilipini
He saw the eldest people from Munupi where they were camping

'Api wiyi awungarri yuwunikijiyarra nginta ngurruwuntakukuwunyi'
    awuta Morruwi
He said, 'I saw those white people, mothers and their children
Pitipamukirigi pipiliyatuwalamigi manya ngawuni
    ngawuntayakuluwunyi'
Come let's go and look for those people'

Ngawa ngajiti wartinga ngawajami yuwurtila mirriparinga
    ngimpirikitimigi
They follow the creek, along the mangroves
Pili nginta ngawunimajajingimami awuta kapi nginayi Murruwi
    Murruntawi, Warlirringa, Marntupula, Kunjirri, Munupula
And their families all those groups ...

Pirimajakirlamira kangi makatinga
They were hiding themselves in the running water

Awungarruwu pirimajapunga arawunikiri awungarri mamurruntawi
    turli pirrijajumwayi
They got to that place and they shot those white people with spears

Wurrumiyanga front beach

Katirrikani

Timber

Katirrikani is the Northern Cypress Pine (*Callitris intratropica*), a tree found among the eucalypt forests in the west of Melville Island. Its wood is traditionally used to make light fishing spears, as a firewood and for its aromatic smoke that helps keep mosquitoes away. Katirrikani also now means timber because its wood was favoured as a building material. Many katirrikani were felled to be hewn for weatherboards, and some of the older Tiwi people remember when the logs were floated along the creeks and down the strait. As children they sat balanced on them while the logs bobbed along in the water. That couldn't be done today for fear of crocodiles.

This song might tell the story of Peter de Hayer, the man remembered for building the church and presbytery that were finished in 1941, but it also follows older songs about logging wood to build houses.

These words were sung by an unidentified senior Tiwi man whose voice was recorded on wax cylinder in 1912.

Pakirrikirri ngimpinjirrikerrayontingini jipurronjinginingiyangirri
I am holding the saw that pushes back and forth

Katirrikani

Parlingarri awarra yati arimurrunta yipurranyumwari ngini ngatawa
Murrakupuni yipirranyuwunga awangurra nguiu
*Long time ago a white man left his country and came to our Country, this place
    here, Lakatinampi.*

Ngarra nguwiriyi ngawa mantani
He went with our friends
Ngini warntirrana awungarra yipamurrumi wutiyati ngawa-rringanuwi
He worked here with our fathers
Ngawa nuka ngintimatangiliparra nuwa
We remember you, we won't forget you

Pukularra murrakupuni pirimajipumuwini
They went into Pukularra Country
Awuta ngarra-rringanuwi amintiya wuta mamirampi
Our fathers and their children
Katirrikani pitirimajingipa
Chopping down the trees
Pika jumajingipurruwami
Using a horse to pull the logs along
Lanjilarra kuluwaga pirrimajingimpingawani
They floated the logs along the creek towards the sea

Anginaki purlawujinga ampijingilirriti
This house is now finished, standing up
Angi ngawa ngampijirramangi
We are living in this house
Pili wuta warntirrana kuripapuranjuwi
They are the people who built that house
Awuta ngawa-rringanuwi amintiya ngawa mantani
Our fathers and their friends

Ngarra jimirrarami Jilyarti
He died there in Darwin
Punuwatumarrimampikupwawurlami jilamarra parratumarrinti
All painting themselves up for mourning and funeral
Parratumampijalipirri parratumampurruwi
We are holding him, we carry him, carry his coffin and we bury him
Ngarikilika nginingajilawula pirlinkiti ngarringimi
We cry together telling this story

Kirilima

Jungle Fowl

Ella Puruntatameri (pictured here), who is an emerging senior songwoman, dances 'Jungle Fowl', and the healing song melody belongs to her family. In the movie *Top End Wedding*, partly filmed on the Tiwi Islands in 2019, the leading character Lauren discovers her Jungle Fowl heritage. The old ladies didn't know this was in the script, but they did know that the actor Miranda Tapsell's Tiwi aunties have Jungle Fowl Dreaming and therefore Miranda should dance Jungle Fowl.

The film's producers asked the ladies for an uplifting song for the final scene when Lauren, who has come to her mother's community for the first time, is sitting watching her Elders dancing and singing 'Jungle Fowl' and welcoming her. Ella led the women in her song that, following traditional song practice, continues her songline and adds new words for the current occasion.

New words marked the day and welcomed the women in Miranda's family, visiting from Darwin, who were going to join in the dancing of 'Jungle Fowl' in this scene. While it was, in a way, staged for the cameras, it was also very much a real Tiwi welcome. So, when you watch the final scene, as the camera pulls out of the post-wedding party and up and over the islands at sunset, you're watching real people and real Tiwi cultural practice.

Kirilima

agha Kurrupuwu - nginta
[Ancestral bird saying] Good morning, this is who I am.

Nginta warriyuwu-jiwati ngunjurru-wiyampirri
    kutuwiyamrramarnipa
*I am your daughter [from Warriyuwu Country], flying
    over and landing here. We see you are up above [like the
    ancestral shooting star], and we stretch out our arms
    to welcome you home*

Wurrumiyanga-jiwati- ngunjurru-wiyampirri
    kutuwiyampi-rranginili
*Our daughter has come back to Wurrumiyanga
    Country. We are all here saying welcome.*

Marranguwula, Warriyuwula, Ranginiwula,
    Jingawula, ngampi Lupwarrinampiwula
Puruntatameri ancestral names and places

Winimingunjimpiyampirru-
    kutuwiyampi rramajirri
We keep telling each other this story

Ahap, kurrawu, kurrupuwu, ayai, nginta

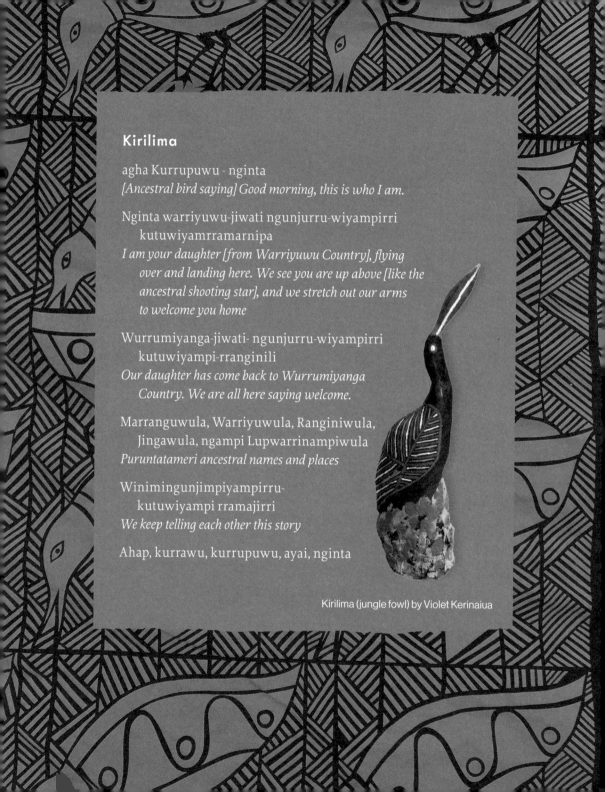

Kirilima (jungle fowl) by Violet Kerinaiua

Jipalangantila amintiya Payapurrurayuwu

A song for the Crocodile people of the Munkara clan

Jipalangantila and Payapurrurayuwu were a senior couple who taught ceremony. This song passes on their message about feeling proud and connected to each other and to Country through the continuation of the songs and dances of Yirrikapayi People. Sung by people of the Munkara clan, Yirrikapayi (Crocodile) People, who are descendants of those two ancestors, as they sing and dance to reaffirm their shared heritage and kinship.

References are made to the ceremonial headdress worn in ceremony by Elders in the past, which are now considered to be symbolic of the deep past knowledge. The words 'true' and 'secret' don't translate exactly but come close to the sense that this knowledge is only known by people who listen properly and learn from the Elders, who learned the stories themselves through the songs and the dances from their Elders long ago. The act of singing this song is a confirmation of cultural heritage, Country and kinship.

Jipalangantila amintiya Payapurrurayuwu

Kurrrukanga wakawayi ngampikangawakawayi

Jipalangantila amintiya Payapurrurayuwu
Jipalangantila and Payapurrurayuwu are singing about Yirrikapayi

Ngawa ninganuwanga ngimpanipingintayi
We still think of you and remember you today
Ngawa kukunari ngimpikujingimi
We are happy and proud
Ngini karri nuwa ngintuwunga awinyirra pukupunyawu
When we wear the headband it symbolises the ancestors and our ties with our
*   Country – it is secret knowledge from long time ago*

Jipirri-kurtawu-rranuwu yartinipirramajirruwa-lapulupa
Jipirri-kurtawu-rranuwu yartinipirramajirruwa-lapulupa pwanki
As we sing, we dance with hands raised up in praise and respect and call out 'peace'

Api ngini ngajingawula ngurrapingintayi
Now everyone is uplifted and happy
Amintiya ngamatapunya awinyirra pirliminga
And we follow the right path in our life
Ngini wuta pirripakuturruwa warntirrana ngirramini
The story they told us was an important message
Pirripamurrumani ngini ngarra ngawa-rringani ngirramini
Our ancestors, our grandfather teaches this story about us

Ngawurrakuruwani ngawa-rringani
We are grateful for our father
Ngini yiwuntamangi yiwuntakturumamigi
They help us and keep us well and strong
Ngawa nginingajingawula ngamatakuluwunyi
We Tiwi people understand the full meaning

Angiwuta pirliminga wuta warntirran mijuwaluwi
They follow their example, those true culture people

Kurrrukanga wakawayi ngampikangawakawayi
Pikilipiyanginila winga winga ampakulumurrigi wuwu
Crocodile ancestor in the mangroves, on the sea, putting out the fire

Jipirri-kurtawu-rranuwu yartinipirramajirruwa-lapulup pwanki
Singing and dancing and call out peace
Wuwu, julup, wuwu, pwanki

[Final...]
Ngawa awungarra ngamirri-ngunjurru-pujingaya-mirratigi
We dance and we sing here, continuing our songline and holding on to their memory

Kulama

Ceremony Song

'We wondered about how to put the words into this book. Part of the song talks about a part of the Kulama ceremony that is really special and only some people can see, some people, only Elders. Not for everybody. Those words we want to put down in our language so that young people can come to us and ask us about that part of Kulama. If they can't understand those old words they can ask us in person, sit down and talk together in person. Keep it special you know?'

Jacinta Tipungwuti

'It's an ongoing thing for young people to carry on and continue the Kulama ceremonies. It belongs to us and we're proud. It's a sacred ritual. It makes people healthy and strong by remembering everything and everyone that came before us.'

Calista Kantilla

This song's introduction is in the traditional musical form for ceremonial Kulama songs created by Carmelina Puantuloura, and was transcribed from a recording of her performance in 1994. The women as a group repeat her words after her, almost as an echo, as they would in ceremony. We sing her words but in our own voice, thinking of our own deceased loved ones. The modern kuruwala style song then begins. Some of this song can't be put into English words.

Japalingini (headband) and
pamajini (armband) for ceremony
by Jacinta Tipungwuti

Kulama

[Kulama solo introduction]
Wakamarrika karri ngimiraninga yinwari-ngilimpangini
Where is my daughter?

Pirlamarri ngirrimili pirlamarri ngirrimili
[the feeling of being uncertain where her spirit has gone, where she sleeps]

Ngarra awungarruwu ngiya rringani yiminikiya manyirramiji
*That's when my dad passed me by. I felt his spirit near me. I felt his presence.
    I am still thinking of him.*

[Modern kuruwala song]
Palingarri ngawa ampi ngawa maningawu ngawa rringanuwi warta
    purruwuriyani
Long time ago our grandfathers and our grandmothers and our fathers went bush

Waya awungarruwu jukuta pirimani ngini awinyirra kulama
There they think about the words they are going to sing in Kulama

Pili ningani wumurrikuwamili
Because today they are ready to sing

Awungarri yikwani marakati pirikuwanyawani
When it's the time of fire, the marakati season, calling out to Country

'Juwa juwa juwa juwa'
[Calling out to their homeland ancestors]

karri waya japinari milimika pirratirikirimani
In the morning the clearing space was made

Yirrimati-kulu-wukari ngini pirratikirumani
They are painting their faces like an owl

Waya awungarri pirratunuwuriyani timilumpulikini
They went with the sharp stick

Ngarawiyaka pinimajakupawulani waya awungarri pirratuwurugani
Kulama yams are taken back to be put on the ground

Kuru-kawanga-wakawayi

Waya yiminga jiyikingarti awungarri mwarliki pirikantirrapurti
When the sun came down, they came up to wash their body

Api waya wuta-mamirampi yintanga puturupurruwani
Then they give names to their children

Wunikijiyapamurla wuta-ampirinyuwi pirriwuntiya-pamulamini
Angi wuta waya yiliyapiga

Angi jajirrima wumunga yikwani pirratikirimani
After three days they made a fire

Waya awungarri ngarawiyaka pitirikijikamini
And then they buried the yams

Api waya awungarri purrukukuni-pirikiringirrani purrukuki,
    purrukuki, purrukuki-yi-a-jayi
*Here I am, leader of Kulama ceremony [the singer takes on the role of the ancestral
    owl man, Purrukukuni, who held the first Kulama ceremony]*

Tumini-pulikini pirratunuwuriyani kangi waya ngarawiyaka
Awungarri wuta mini yatiwi yintanga putupurrani
Nginta waya Ayipa Wimami api waya awungarri
Awurankini yintanga wurupurrigani wuta mamirampi
Ngajingawula yoi ngamirrikujuwurtumi awinyirra ngawarripwaka
Japinari jipakiyayi watirimi wurrinyini
Watirikinyawu waya awungarri ngimpatuwapa awinyirra ngarawiyaka
Api watirimarimi-yajirri kapi wutawa tangarima

*[They dance for their families, their skingroups and their country groups and then
    this is the end of the Kulama ceremony.]*

Kuru-kawanga-wakawayi

Ngawa naringa nyirra pupuka

Oh pure and bright

We sing this song together for healing. The melody comes from an old hymn 'Oh Pure and Bright', which we sang as young girls in the mission school. The Tiwi words are not a direct translation of that hymn, but they are our words about how we see Our Lady. We have that same feeling of motherhood and so that song makes us feel, like her, how she felt for her son. We are the women feeling the same as her, the gentle caring mother, so we ask her to heal us and help us let the worries lift up from us.

Ngawa naringa nyirra pupuka

Ngawa naringa ngawa naringa tayamangi ngawa tayikuwapi
Tamarriripa kangawula kirijini (Jesus), pili ngawa mijuwalini
Ngawa ngaringa nyirra pupuka, ngawa-yuwuni nyirra mwartingarra
    yimulungurrumi
Ngawa-naringa ngawa-ngampurukuwani pili nyirra pupuka
Tayamangi kapi purunjuwi amintiya kapi pupuwi

*Our mother, beautiful lady, our lady who holds us in your heart, as you hold
    your baby, Jesus, our hearts lift up in our love.*

Molly

Ngawa ngirimika

We are family

'*As Sistagirls, we join singing and dancing in men's or women's roles just the same as everybody. Our physical gender and our identity are not as important in ceremony as kinship, just the same as for all Tiwi people.*'

Bertram Tipungwuti and Ainsley Kerinaiua

When we went to Mardi Gras in Sydney we had two groups – 'traditional' and 'traditional contemporary'. We went down to Tiwi Design to choose the fabrics. The 'traditional contemporary' group chose the sea, Jabiru, Pukumani pole, Pamajini, dragonfly, sea shell – all traditional designs but in rainbow colours to celebrate the LGBTQIA+ community. The 'traditional' group chose fabric with the other designs, wearing dresses and nagas, Pamijini, Japalingini, painted up with ochre and carrying spears and tawutawunga. For some extra sparkle we all had bud lights wound around us. We all danced our Yoi as we went down Oxford Street in the parade.

We sang traditional Tiwi culture songs that we had arranged together in a dance remix. The old ladies asked us to compose a new song especially to be included in this book and we are proud to be part of the song culture of our islands.'

Ngawa ngirimika

Najingawula ngaruwanajirri ngini waya ngawa mantawi ngini
awurrayamangi ngini-ngawula murrakupuni najingawula kukunari
kapi ngawa-yuwupi, ngawa-rringanuwi, ngawa-ampiyi karri waya
yurupini Kulama.
*We participate in community and we help support the Elders by collecting food
from Country when they are preparing for Kulama*

Ngajingawula kukunari ngarimi karri kuwayi wurumi kangawula ngini
ngawiyarti Yoyi ngarimajirri amintiya ngamungurumi ngalami ngini
awarra yintanga kapi Kulama.
*We are proud to be involved in culture, in Yoi ceremony and in Kulama ceremony
because it is part of who we are*

Kapi awungarru murrakupuni Sydney ngawa awungaji yoyi
ngintirikirimi ngini wuta ngawa-ampi ngawa-rringanwui yoyi pirimani
*We showcased our culture at Mardi Gras and at the Minyarli Festival and at
Putanga, Jabiru side*

Ngawatuwu awunuwanga yoyi
ngarimi karri ngawa-mantawi
yupurrarami, ngajingawula
putuputuwu ngarimajirri kapi
ngawa-ngirimipi amintiya
ngamantawi
*We held ceremony for our own
departed family and friends*

Ngawa awungarri papuranjuwi
amintiya kukunari ngarimi
ngawulamiya pili ngawa papuranjuwi ngawa-mantawi
We are strong and proud of who we are

Wuta waya kukunari kangawula pili ngawayarti ngampangira tiwi
ngirrami amintiya yoyi ngarimi kapi nginingawula milimika
They can see who we are as young Tiwi Sistagirls living here

Ngarikuruwala nginingawula murrakupuni

We sing about our Country

This song brings us Tiwi Islanders all together, as we call out to all of the Countries. We are proud of our ancestors and our people as Traditional Owners and the ties we have to those Countries. Our children and grandchildren will become those Custodians of the land in the future.

Ngarikuruwala nginingawula murrakupuni

Nginaki nginingawula murrakupuni yuwurrara ratuwati
This is our land the two islands

Ngini ngawa ngarukuruwala nginingawula murrakupuni
We are singing about our land

Kapi wuta ngawa-ampi ngawa tangarima yimamini
It is from our ancestors who lived in that land

Wuta wangatajirri tangarima atumujinguma
They are all belonging to their own homeland

Jamulampi, Yayimpi, Wulurankuwu
Munupi, Malawu,Wurrankuwu amintiya Jikilarruwu
Nginingawula murrakupuni
We call out to our Country ... Our Country

Ngawatuwu wiyi awungarri ngamantirranyuwiya
When are we going to go there [we feel drawn to go there]

Kapi wuta ngawa-ampi tangarima yimamini
To our ancestors' homeland

Arrami awungaji warntarrana yartipuranji
True, good land it's a beautiful Country

Wuta nguwuri wuta nguwuri awuta ngawa-ampi
We pay respects to our ancestors when we go back to our homeland

Ngawa ngumpunyukuruwarni nginja ngirringani
We each sing and celebrate to thank our father

Ngini nginja jimantakirayi nginingawula murrakupuni
That he passed down to us our beautiful Country

Jamulampi, Yayimpi, Wulurangkuwu, Munupi, Malawu, Wurangkuwu,
Jikilaruwu ngingawula pupuni murrakupuni
[Sing out to our beautiful Country]

Kapi ngawa Tiwi

We are all Tiwi

Marie Simplicia Tipuamantimerri taught us this song. We always sing it with our grandchildren when we are sitting with them and having a singalong. Everybody knows the words and we all sing it together at community gatherings, like special events at school or when important visitors come. The clapping hands together is good for them to start to learn to hear Tiwi music and to dance.

Kapi ngawa Tiwi

Kapi ngawa Tiwi awungarra ngawurrakiriparra amintiya yoyi
    ngawurrami
We are the Tiwi all here clapping and dancing

Pili ngawa yati murrakupuni amintiya yati ngampangira
That is because we all live in one Tiwi Country and speak our Tiwi language

Ngawurrakiriparra, ngawurrakiriparri ngininganjingawula
Clap, clap everyone

Awungarra nguiu
Right here in our Tiwi land

Mamanta kukunari ngawurrami ngawa ngarjirti jirti ngarumuwu wajirri
Everyone love each other and feel very happy

Pilingawa yati murrakupuni amintiya yati ngampangira
We speak one language and live together in one land

OUR COLLABORATION

I first heard Tiwi Kuruwala songs in 2007, and quickly fell in love with them and with the wonderful elderly women who sing them – the Wangatunga Strong Women's Group. There was something about the sound of their voices and the way they blended cultures that fascinated me. I took myself up north and introduced myself to the most senior women of the group, with a then vague idea of wanting to make music with them in some way. We spent those first few days sitting under a tree as the old ladies split and wove their pandanus, passing the day with stories and singing, and I listened. Slowly I built up the courage to play along with them a little on my horn. We hit it off and got excited about the prospect of sharing the women's songs with a wider audience, and they were keen to explore adding some instrumental backing to their vocals.

Within a few months Teresita Puruntatameri and I had approached the Darwin Festival with an idea for a collaborative performance bringing Tiwi and non-Tiwi music together to see where it led us. We formed the group Ngarukuruwala (We Sing) for our first performance at the festival in August that year. Since then, the old ladies and I have been meeting up whenever we can to sit and talk, share stories and sing and play. We have performed and recorded together whenever we have the opportunity, with the aim being to share musical ideas and create new versions of old songs, for fun and entertainment, but also for the women, with the firm purpose of keeping their songs alive.

Before I met the Tiwi women, I knew very little about First Nations music and nothing about the Tiwi Islands. I was a freelance musician, having played

in the orchestras for musical theatre, opera, touring concerts and television. Living and working in Sydney, I started to juggle family and freelance work with trips up north, funded by small arts grants aimed at recording the songs that the senior Tiwi women and men wanted to preserve.

In 2009, eleven Tiwi elders and I visited the Australian Institute of Aboriginal and Torres Strait Islander Studies in Canberra to reclaim field recordings of Tiwi songs, collected by anthropologists over the last century, the earliest made by Baldwin Spencer in 1912. This was a significant and moving experience for the group as they heard the recorded voices of great-grandfathers, mothers and even their younger selves for the first time. The repatriation of this material has informed all our collaborative work since then, including this book, and has had a great impact in the community as the Elders use it to maintain ceremony and language.

As I learned more about Tiwi song types and their ceremonial, social and cultural functions and the complexities of the melodies and the song texts, I found myself becoming a researcher as well as a musician. The women also became researchers as well as singers, passing on their knowledge – both of song practice and of the deep-past ancestral lore that is held in the texts. This work led to my PhD, which presents the first written transcription and analysis of the twelve classical Tiwi song melodies. Our most recent projects continue to involve performance and cultural preservation and the creation of new music with the documentation of traditional composition practice. We are always finding new ways to maintain Tiwi sung heritage and knowledge transmission.

The Strong Women's Group has performed at the Darwin Festival and the Sydney Festival, at the Australian National Gallery, the Sydney Opera House and the Sydney Recital Hall. In collaboration with non-Tiwi jazz and classical musicians, they have led re-workings of some of their songs in musical styles that they enjoy and that have embraced and expanded the musical knowledge and skills of all of us involved. In 2008 the women sang at the final celebratory Mass of World Youth Day, given by Pope Benedict XVI, for an audience of 400,000 people (and likely many thousands more via international broadcast). Considering the entire Tiwi population is around 2,500, it was an extraordinary moment and one the women took in their stride, with no hint of nervousness nor a falter in their performance.

As ambassadors for their culture and community, they have performed and presented seminars with me at musicology and language conferences around Australia, and have run a number of youth-focused music projects in their community as well as recording Tiwi songs in old ways and new.

Whether on stage or not, at the heart of the women's singing is always their desire to share the stories and bring people together through the songs. At home, singing for healing for their Tiwi family and singing that same healing song for someone they had only just met and heard was unwell. Dancing their Yoi on the Tantipi beach just for fun, for themselves, after a day of collecting mussels, and dancing Crocodile, Shark and Rainbow under the sails of the Opera House, bringing their ancestors on the 6,000-kilometre journey. It is all the same: the songs are who they are.

Ngarukuruwala has developed into much more than a 'show' or a 'project'. It is a group of people – Tiwi singers, Elders and increasingly also younger women and men, and non-Tiwi classical and jazz musicians – who come together occasionally to make new music. It is also the ongoing bond between the ladies and me, with the preservation of an endangered piece of Australia's artistic heritage at the core of everything we do together.

Genevieve Campbell
2022

Clementine, Genevieve, Judith and Leonie

Cultural respect

For Tiwi people, the restriction on using an image of a deceased person, their name, their recorded voice or their song is lifted once that person has had their Yiloti Pukumani – around one year after death. The names, images and voices of women who have died are included in this book with the permission of family, who are proud to honour their memory and cultural legacy in this way. As others will sadly pass away in the future, we ask that you treat this book and audio with sensitivity.

Note about the songs

Some of the songs in this book were first printed in the *Nguiu Mother's Club Eisteddfod Songbook*, printed by the Literacy Production Centre, Nguiu, 1994. For their inclusion here they have been reconsidered and some words and phrases have been updated by the women. Some more personal or occasion-specific references have been removed or rewritten to make the songs available to a wider audience and create a useful resource for future Tiwi singers.

Contributors

Calista Kantilla, Jacinta Tipungwuti, Leonie Tipiloura, Mary Elizabeth Moreen, Regina Kantilla, Augusta Punguatji, Molly Munkara, Marie-Carmel Kantilla, Gregoriana Parker, Della Kerinaiua, Rachel Woody, Nina Black, Frances Therese Portaminni, Marcella Fernando, Francis Orsto, Ella Puruntatameri, Marie Simplicia Tipuamantimirri, Carol Puruntatameri, Shirley Puruntatameri, Sheba Fernando, Rosemary Tipungwuti, Gemma Munkara, Ainsley Kerinaiua, Bertram Tipungwuti

With thanks also to

John Louis Munkara, Virginia Garlala, Alberta Puruntatameri, Cathy Stassi, Jedda Puruntatameri, Marius Puruntatameri, Tony Pilakui, Doriana Bush, Pam Brook, Judith Puruntatameri, Jocelyn Black, Annalisa Warlampinni, Aileen Puruntatameri, Shirley Puruntatameri, Fiona Kerinaiua, Maggie Tipungwuti, Anne Marie Puruntatameri, Ancilla Puruntatameri

In memory of contributors who have passed

Teresita Puruntatameri, Eunice Orsto, Concepta Orsto, Casmira Munkara, Clementine Puruntatameri, Cynthia Portaminni, Eugenie Tipungwuti, Eustace Tipiloura

Credits

Photo credits

Simon Bartlett: 54
Genevieve Campbell: ii, iv, vi, 3, 12, 15, 31, 34, 35, 36, 51, 58, 59, 60, 61, 63, 65, 68, 73, 76, 78, 80, 81, 83, 86, 87, 88, 90, 93, 94, 96, 97, 102,108,109, 111, 112, 113, 114, 117, 122, 128, 133, 138, 139, 140, 148, 149, 151, 156, 162, 165, 166, 169, 170, 172, 175, 180, 185, 187
Helen Campbell: 137, 191
Bruce Cartwright: 23, 74, 77, 106, 154
Avani Dias: 182
Nathaniel Fay: 48, 142
William Hall: 28, 40
Diane Moore: 36, 38, 163
Fiona Morrison: 16, 44, 53, 67, 150
Jillian Mundy: 4, 99, 142
Tiffany Parker: 133
Patajikiyali Museum: 70, 146
Roger Press: 9, 144, 167, 188
Shane Tipuamantamerri: 18
Prudence Upton: 41, 99, 148
Courtesy Bertram Tipungwuti: 183
Matthew WF Wells, Goodwell Productions: 181
Celina Whan, courtesy AFL Northern Territory Media (2022): 130, 131, 133
Photographs (taken in 1928) by Charles Hart, courtesy Macleay Museum collection, Chau Chak Wing Museum, University of Sydney: 126
Photographs (taken in 1948) by Axel Poignant, courtesy National Library of Australia: 125, 127

Fabric courtesy Tiwi Designs

Kulama ceremony by Marie Josette Orsto: Cover
Jilamara (paint), by Jeanne Baptiste Apuatimi: 59, 124, 188
Pandanus, by Osmond Kantilla: endpapers, iv, chapter openers, 28, 84
Tuninga (lizard), by Natalie Tungutalum: 137

DEDICATION

We would like to pay our respects to members of the Strong Women's Group who have passed away. These women worked together with us and they were always there for us, showing us the way. What we know today and how we make our songs is all because of them. Although they have passed away, we still hear their voices in our recordings and we hear them calling out to welcome us into our Country now that their spirits have returned there.

As Elders they showed their love for the community, encouraging people to be proud of our language and our culture. Now we carry the knowledge we collected from them. We forget words, it's like the sea returning with the tide, their words flow back to us.

'We are still living. We have that knowledge from these women. We are five Elders now. The most important thing about Elders is to be listening to each other. We try to teach people about being gentle with each other. We are still doing that, some of us. Joy and happiness, happy hunting, sharing, dancing, giving food to each other. We sing out in the bush, collecting pandanus, we come back and we sing together as we weave. That's all we can do today. People have their ups and downs and problems. We are here to help them let it go. We are the ones, the leaders in the Community. We are good role models for the young people coming up. No matter if we are hurting, we always have compassion and love for each other. We have to show them how to look after each other and work together.' **Jacinta Tipungwuti**

Murli la

SONGS AND STORIES OF THE TIWI ISLANDS

NGARUKURUWALA WOMEN'S GROUP
with GENEVIEVE CAMPBELL

Cover artwork: Kulama ceremony fabric design by Marie Josette Orsto
Cover photograph: Leonie Tipiloura, Jacinta Tipungwuti and Calista Kantilla
dancing Ampiji (Rainbow) at the Festival of Sydney, 2016.

Indigenous
Literacy
Foundation

Hardie Grant
EXPLORE